Dancing
with
Our Selves

Dancing
with
Our Selves

A PRACTICAL GUIDE TO HARNESS THE EGO AND LIVE ON PURPOSE

BRITTANY HOPKINS SWITLICK

For more information contact dancingwithourselves@gmail.com.
ISBN: 979-8-89316-354-4 - paperback
ISBN: 979-8-89316-355-1 - hardcover
ISBN: 979-8-89316-353-7 - ebook

Get The Workbook For Free!

To say thank you for reading my book, I would like to give you the *Dancing with Our Selves* companion workbook 100 percent FREE!

I have found readers who download and use the <u>Dancing with Our Selves Workbook PDF</u> implement the work faster and take the next steps needed to navigate the dance between their ego and higher self.

You can get a copy by visiting:
<u>www.brittanyhopkins.com</u>

To my children—Isaac and Vinni—may you always know yourselves and speak your truths with love and compassion.

Contents

Foreword..11

Introduction: The Dance of the Ego and Higher Self.................15

Chapter 1: Name it to Tame it...................................... **25**

   Practice #1: Name Your Ego.......................................*40*

   Practice #2: Acknowledge How You're Feeling....................*42*

Chapter 2: Dear Ego Self... **45**

   Practice #3: I'm Breathing in, and I'm Breathing out Meditation 57

   Practice #4: Letter to Your Ego Self..............................*60*

   Practice #5: It Makes Sense That You Feel.........................*64*

Chapter 3: It's Mostly Lies.. **68**

   Practice #6: Identify Your Limiting Beliefs, or Lies..............*85*

   Practice #7: Identify Your Ego Statements........................*94*

   Practice #8: Create Your Empowered Statements..................*100*

Chapter 4: The Drama of Life..................................... **105**

   Practice #9: What Does Your Ego Tend to Say in Drama?...........*120*

   Practice #10.1: Identify Your Drama..............................*142*

   Practice #10.2: Exaggerate Your Current Attitude.................*144*

   Practice #10.3: What if.....*145*

   Practice #10.4: Drastically Change Your Posture and

     Breathe on Purpose *147*

   Practice #10.5: Heart-Centered Gratitude *148*

   Practice #10.6: Get Curious......................................*150*

   Practice #10.7: Claim Responsibility *151*

   Practice #10.8: Let Go *152*

   Practice #10.9: Accountability...................................*154*

Chapter 5:   The Ongoing Journey **159**
Practice #11: Reflecting on the Gifts of Your Ego........................*163*
Practice #12: The Dance of Competency *166*
Part 1: Competency Awareness *166*
Part 2: Competency and Limiting Beliefs *166*
Part 3: Navigating Competence using The Drama
  Triangle and The Empowerment Dynamic............................*167*
Practice #13: Seven-Day Self-Care Routine..............................*171*

References *181*

FOREWORD

By Tevara Paranto, LCSW

As a licensed clinical social worker and psychotherapist with over twenty years of experience, I've dedicated my career to helping people heal their inner wounds and reconnect with their authentic selves. My healing journey began in my teens, fostering a deep appreciation for therapy, mindfulness, and practices that support personal growth. Years later, yoga became a profound part of that journey, offering me a way to unite my body and mind that was transformative.

In the summer of 2023, I registered for yoga teacher training to deepen my yoga practice. I envisioned learning to guide students through poses, sequences, and the beautiful flow of asanas. I looked forward to exploring yoga philosophy and studying pranayama. I received all of that—and more. What I didn't expect was how much the training, facilitated by Brittany, would mirror the inner healing work I've dedicated my life to. It provided practical tools that transformed my understanding of myself and became powerful resources I now use with my clients.

Brittany has a beautiful ability to make the abstract tangible and immediately applicable. Her approach blends ancient yogic teachings with modern, real-world tools for self-discovery.

Her compassionate yet incisive guidance allowed me to recognize the intricate dance we perform between our ego and higher selves—and that the ego self isn't something to vanquish but to understand and integrate as we connect with our higher selves.

As a psychotherapist, I was struck by how deeply this work reflects the essence of therapy itself:

- Becoming present.
- Identifying the core beliefs, like who we think we should be, what we must achieve, and how we ought to show up in the world, that may no longer serve us.
- Creating new, more empowering ways forward.

Brittany's process of recognizing and working with the ego captures the heart of healing—it's about reclaiming the truth of who we are beyond the stories and illusions that hold us back.

Using the tools Brittany shares, I've learned to soothe and work with my ego self, which I lovingly call 'Little Tevara,' instead of letting her lead the dance of my life. Similarly, each chapter in this book offers practical tools to shine a light on your ego self, compassionately keep it in check, and invite your higher self to take the lead.

These insights will help you navigate the dance between your ego and higher self with intention and compassion.

The best part? While I highly recommend it, you don't need to have ever stepped foot on a yoga mat, or in a yoga studio, to benefit from the practices in this book. These tools are practical and accessible for anyone ready to explore and gain clarity, balance, and authenticity.

Dancing with Our Selves: A Practical Guide to Harness the Ego and Live On Purpose is a gift—a road map for confronting the ego's illusions and rediscovering your true self. Brittany doesn't just teach yoga; she holds space for self-exploration and transformation, where you feel empowered to meet yourself with compassion and curiosity. Her guidance goes beyond the mat, offering tools that ripple into every area of life—helping you navigate challenges, cultivate presence, and step into your higher self with confidence. I'm endlessly grateful to have been her student and thrilled to see her wisdom shared on these pages.

May this book inspire, challenge, and guide you to step boldly into the dance with your ego and higher self, bringing more presence, purpose, and joy to your life.

With gratitude and love,

Tevara Paranto.
Licensed Clinical Social Worker and Psychotherapist

The Dance of the Ego and Higher Self

Imagine life as a dance where two partners are in constant motion. In just about any partner dance, someone typically takes the lead, guiding the flow and direction of the movement. In the dance with our selves, we would ideally let our wise, mature, and creative higher self guide us, and often it does. Unfortunately, when we're tired, hungry, stressed, or threatened, we typically let the immature, reactive, and dramatic ego self take the lead. Since the dance isn't a solo, each partner must bring their unique energy and perspective to the movement. To create a harmonious dance, we must learn to harness the ego's dynamic qualities while allowing the higher self to take the lead.

This dynamic between our higher self and ego is rooted in the web of our complex psychological development. To take a complicated concept and put it into a very small nutshell; the ego self begins to develop in early childhood, influenced by a combination of biological, psychological, and social factors. It continues to evolve throughout life as we adapt to various situations. It provides us with unconscious habits and reactive states. It overuses familiar patterns and wears out our dance shoes unevenly.

Our ego self is trying to help us prioritize safety, control, and the validation of long-held beliefs, which can limit our growth and potential. This partner's movements, while essential to the dance, are often rooted in past experiences and future anxieties, causing us to act out of fear, defensiveness, or a need to prove ourselves.

The other partner, our higher self, embodies a different rhythm and energy. This partner moves with grace, purpose, and conscious intention, acting with deep preference in the present moment. When the higher self takes the lead, the dance becomes a beautiful expression of our true essence in combination with the personality flourishes the ego self brings into our lives.

The higher self guides us to act from a place of presence and compassion, allowing us to respond thoughtfully to life's challenges rather than reacting impulsively. In this dance, we're more attuned to our authentic desires and more empathetic toward others, creating a fulfilling life.

The dynamic of which part of ourselves takes the lead in this dance can change moment by moment. It requires awareness and practice to recognize when our ego self is dominating and to consciously invite our higher self to step forward in the partnership. By learning to discern these shifts and intentionally choosing to follow the higher self's lead, we can transform the dance from one of survival to one of thriving.

This book will provide you with the tools and insights needed to make this shift, empowering you to dance through life with confidence and purpose.

If Dancing is Not Your Thing

Visualize yourself driving a car with two familiar passengers in the back seat—your ego self and your higher self. To the outside world, it looks like you are in control, driving the car. But in reality, these two backseat passengers are constantly offering their input. The ego self often takes charge, loudly directing where to go, what to say, and how to react, sometimes triggering nervous system responses that feel out of your control.

The ego self has been with you for as long as you can remember, shaping your responses based on past experiences and survival instincts. It's a natural part of who you are, but when it tries to backseat drive, it can lead to reactions that don't always serve your highest good. The higher self, on the other hand, is also there in the back seat, quietly offering guidance that's more aligned with your true values, purpose, and long-term well-being. Unfortunately, it's often overshadowed by the louder, more reactive ego self.

Now, imagine inviting both the reactive and conscious parts of yourself to move to the front seats—the ego self in the passenger seat and the higher self in the driver's seat. With this shift, the ego is still present, still offering its insights, but it no longer dictates your every move. Instead, your higher self is now in control, guiding the car with clarity, purpose, and conscious choice.

While driving, the higher self is stoic, determined and unfazed by the whims of the ego. Seeing that their tricks won't work, the ego adjusts and becomes an ally. From the passenger seat, the ego self helps you recognize your preferences, aversions, and reminders of past experiences and how far you've come. With the higher self driving, the ego becomes a support system instead of a distraction, allowing you to navigate your life in a way that's mindful and aligned with your true self.

Who is this book for?

Recognizing the interplay between these two aspects of yourself, this book is designed to help you navigate that relationship. You might be doing well in life. You might be a full-fledged adult with lots of useful skills. You're probably good at your job, too. You might be a loving friend, partner, or parent. Likely, you've spent much of your life looking like more than enough to the outside world, yet feeling like you're *not good enough* on a good day and like a complete failure on the worst days. You desperately want to feel good in your skin—both physically and emotionally.

If you look back at your life and wonder why you made certain choices or keep repeating the same self-sabotaging behaviors, telling yourself, "I *should* be different. I *should* know better," then this book is for you.

You will keep repeating your patterns unless you take action. The good news is you're reading this book, so you are confirming that you are ready for action now.

If you are open to the tools shared in each chapter, you'll recognize the ways you may unconsciously be holding yourself back. You will gain a better understanding of yourself and a deeper sense of compassion for those around you. All of your relationships will benefit from this process, starting with the relationship with yourself.

An Overview of What You'll Discover

The strategies I share come from various backgrounds and have been tested and proven to work for thousands of people. I have used all of these strategies, not just in my own life, but also as part of the ego work in the 200-hour and 300-hour yoga teacher trainings I lead.

My graduates repeatedly share that getting to know their ego self has transformed their lives and relationships with their kids and partners, family and friends, coworkers and clients.

Each chapter builds on key principles that will help you shine light on your ego self, and understand how to keep it in check, while inviting your higher self to take the lead more of the time. Chapter 1 will be about getting present to yourself in the 'now here' moment. My longtime teacher, Baron Baptiste, says, "You're either *now here* or you are *nowhere*." Our egos spend so much time holding on to habits from the past or worrying about the future that we're lost—we're *nowhere*.

From the present moment, you can intentionally reflect on your life for clues on how and why your ego self developed the way it did. Through the practices in Chapter 2, you will have more compassion for your ego. With compassion, you will more easily step out of unconscious reaction and choose instead to be in action in life, with your higher self taking the lead.

Once you can see your reactive ego self and start talking about it in the third person, you'll be able to recognize the things it tries to tell you that limit how you show up in the world. The teachings and practices in Chapter 3 will support you in seeing how you may unconsciously try to prove what the ego says as 'right' or 'wrong.' These unconscious habits drain your energy, and instead of doing things because you *can*, you do things because you *should*. You will also explore your ego's reactive ego statements and choose instead to create empowered statements that set you up for success in challenging moments.

Two of my favorite tools for identifying whether I'm letting my ego or higher self take the lead are offered in Chapter 4: The Drama Triangle and The Empowerment Dynamic®. When I'm feeling powerless or not at peace, I know my ego self is playing the role of victim, rescuer, or persecutor. Like many things, seeing the problem is the first step.

Once you recognize yourself in the drama, you can then choose to shift into the energy of the creator, coach, or challenger at any time. As the latter, you're in the present moment and can feel all authentic feelings without resistance, no matter what shows up in your life.

Last but not least, in Chapter 5, you'll be invited to see where in your life you naturally operate from your higher self consistently and why it sometimes feels so easy. On the flip side, you'll see where and why in your life you default to letting your ego take the lead. I will invite you to see how powerful it can be to make small daily choices that support you in showing up as your best self.

My goal is for you to have discoveries in every chapter that transform how you show up in the world. I hope that you find what is shared so profoundly useful that you can't help but talk about it with everyone in your life and invite them to join you in reading this book. The more we can all recognize when our ego selves are in reaction and, instead, shift into action as our higher selves, the more enjoyable the dance of life will be.

Perspective

As you navigate the tools and concepts in this book, it's important to remember that most of the insights shared here are based on my personal use of the tools and concepts. The stories I write are shaped by the environments I've lived in and the experiences I've had as a cisgender white woman raised in the U.S. I grew up in a small town in Texas, attended a liberal arts college in the midwest, and have traveled to Nepal, India, Japan, Thailand, Canada, and Europe. I lived abroad in England as a child and in Beijing, China, as an adult.

After retiring from the professional dance world, I drove a car that ran on waste vegetable oil, lived in a straw bale house I co-built, and created dance programs at two international boarding schools before moving to Colorado to open a yoga studio. I was in a sixteen-year relationship and marriage that began when I was twenty-four; we had a kid at thirty-eight and divorced at forty. I remarried at forty-two and had a second child at forty-three. These experiences have influenced my worldview, teachings, and how I approach personal growth and spirituality.

The point is, the stories and lessons in this book are simply my perspective. Take what resonates with you, and leave the rest. If there are things that rub you the wrong way, my hope is that you can stay open to see what does land for you and still have discoveries that support your growth and evolution.

How to Use This Book

As you move through this book, enjoy reading the stories I share—many of which are quite embarrassing or humbling moments from my own life when I've been operating from my ego self. (I've changed some details and names to protect others' privacy.) Along the way, you'll also learn the background for various tools and practices that are helpful in shifting into more empowered ways of being.

Please don't just read and cross your fingers, hoping the lessons will sink in. I encourage you to challenge yourself to actually do the journaling exercises as they come up. It will be worth the time and effort. And remember, as we say in the yoga world, "It's a practice, not a perfect."

You can use any journal that feels good to you. Personally, I love the Day One journaling app. To make it easy for you to stay engaged with the exercises, there is also a PDF of all the practices available for free download on my website at www.brittanyhopkins.com.

The Devious Devil and the Judgmental Angel

It's expected to feel a little like a bag of mixed nuts at the beginning of any new line of self-inquiry. You may feel curious, skeptical, nervous, excited, or any number of other feelings.

So often, the people I work with start to recognize their ego and immediately blame or try to reject that part of themselves. It's almost as if their ego creates another layer, where the ego gets an ego. It's like having a devious devil on one shoulder, whispering lies in one ear, and a judgy angel on the other, harshly criticizing every move.

This internal tug-of-war creates even more resistance. Instead of finding clarity, it pushes you further away from balance and self-compassion, trapping you in a cycle where neither side allows space for understanding or healing. When these opposing voices dominate, it becomes harder to approach yourself with kindness and create the harmony you're seeking.

Have you ever experienced this battle within yourself? If so, what does it feel like in your body? Does it feel like tightness in your chest, a knot in your stomach, or tension in your shoulders? Pay attention to these sensations as they come up in the reading of this book—they can be clues about how your ego is showing up in the moment. The practices and tools I share will help you navigate these feelings and create balance.

For those of you familiar with the first two limbs of yoga, I invite you to bring in the yamas and niyamas to your process. Ahimsa (non-harming) guides us to approach ourselves with kindness, while Satya (truthfulness) helps us get real about how we're showing up. Asteya (non-stealing) reminds us not to rob ourselves of balance by overexerting or underexerting, and Brahmacharya (moderation) keeps us from extremes. Aparigraha (non-possessiveness) invites us to let go of attachment to outcomes. Saucha (purity) cultivates clarity, Santosha (contentment) teaches us to accept where we are, and Tapas (discipline) fuels our commitment to stay in the discomfort to get to the transformation. Svadhyaya (self-study) drives our inner reflection, and Ishvara Pranidhana (surrender) reminds us to trust the process. Together, these principles create a balanced, compassionate approach to the ego work in this book.

Please offer yourself grace. Your ego is trying to show you what you love, fear, want, and need. Keep reading, and you'll find yourself dancing like never before—moving through life with clarity and energy.

CHAPTER 1

Name it to Tame it

Growing up in the '80s and '90s meant Saturday morning cartoons, big hair, mixtapes, and landlines. I played the original Nintendo with my brothers and can watch home videos of our constantly shifting family dynamic—if I can find a VHS player. I was a latchkey kid, choreographing dances in the garage to Janet Jackson in grade school and rocking out to The Cure and Indigo Girls in high school, all before the arrival of dial-up internet.

Life was both colorful and complicated. I was three when my parents divorced, and by the time I was six, both parents had remarried. In what seemed like overnight, I was the second youngest child and only girl among six brothers, split between two very different households.

Looking back, I know to the core of my being I was loved deeply. My passion for dance was nurtured and supported by my parents, and I was given countless opportunities to learn, grow, laugh, and play. Alongside the good that was my childhood, I needed to develop coping strategies to navigate the complexities that come along with the human experience. I learned to stay quiet when necessary, be overly agreeable, work really hard, and manipulate to maintain harmony and safety. These strategies were necessary and helped me survive the emotional roller coaster of my first eighteen years. Unfortunately, as the ego clings to what seems to work, these childhood coping mechanisms evolved into unconscious, reactive ego behaviors that often hold me back as an adult.

My ego-driven patterns have hindered many of my relationships, particularly in my first marriage to Derek. I didn't fully recognize this dynamic until one day in 2019, during a conversation with my best friend, Mollie.

Mollie was living in Alaska at the time, and I was in Colorado. We'd been close since 2010, sharing a bond as yoga teachers and teacher training facilitators. I vividly remember telling her, "I feel like I'm one person with two parts. There's the confident and happy version of me with my friends, creating the yoga community within my studio and teaching yoga. Then there's this self-sabotaging part of myself that has dominated how I show up in my marriage."

Mollie listened thoughtfully, as she always does, and then posed a question that changed everything. "What if you named the self-sabotaging part of yourself?"

"What do you mean?" I asked, curious but a little skeptical.

"Give your ego a name," she suggested. "It might help you create enough distance to observe and understand why you self-sabotage."

I paused to think about it. "Like what? What kind of name?"

"How about Brandi?" Mollie said with a chuckle. "Brandi with an 'i'."

I laughed, feeling a spark of clarity. "Yes! Brandi with a heart over the 'i', like we did in middle school!"

It was a lightbulb moment. We laughed and talked about all the ways Brandi showed up in my life.

As we chatted, I said, "I can feel vital, clear, capable, and fun in one moment, and Derek will say something, look at me a certain way, or even just walk by without a word, and everything changes.

Brandi is so concerned with looking good, being needed, and avoiding conflict that my body will instantly feel tight in the chest and nauseous in the stomach. I'll get the overwhelming need to do something, anything, to feel better—even if it means self-sacrificing at almost every turn."

I could feel Mollie nodding through the phone. "Exactly. By naming her, you can start to see when she takes over and maybe even have some compassion because she's trying to help you."

Over the next five years, Brandi remained a constant companion. I navigated the divorce from Derek when our son, Isaac, was two years old. I sold the yoga studio building and transitioned my teaching business online. Brandi and I danced together through the beginning of a surprising new relationship with my now husband, Adam—which led to the birth of our daughter, Vinni.

Through it all, Brandi was—and is—the part of me that reacts in moments of stress or conflict. She shows up most often when I'm tired and overwhelmed—when my executive brain functions struggle to stay on board. When my energetic gas tank light comes on, Brandi takes the wheel, driving me into reaction mode instead of thoughtful action.

An example of this happened not long ago, on a day when I had completely overbooked myself. I was juggling work, family, and household responsibilities when I got a call from school letting me know that Isaac, our six-year-old, was sick and needed to be picked up. The added task felt like the tipping point. In an instant, Brandi showed up. Instead of calmly figuring out how to manage the shift in the day, I huffed at Adam, aggressively grabbed my purse and keys, and rushed out the door to pick up Isaac feeling emotionally out of control.

I was tired and overwhelmed, and Brandi's reaction was to let everyone know just how burdened I felt. It wasn't until later that I realized how much stress had fueled my overreaction, turning what could have been a simple change of plans into an emotional, egotistical storm.

Rewiring the Idea of Egotistical

Our culture often lumps the ego into a single, not-so-flattering box. Terms like "egotistical" and "narcissistic" are frequently used interchangeably, painting a picture of someone who is arrogant. Google's AI defines egotistical as "excessively conceited or absorbed in oneself; self-centered," with examples like, "He's selfish, egotistical, and arrogant."

But what if we could rewire how we think about being egotistical? The traditional definition captures part of the story of what it looks or feels like to be self-absorbed, but not the whole story. Yes, for some, the ego self thinks they're better than others. However, for other people, the ego self may be hyper-focused on thinking they need to prove their worth or that they're less than others. So, what if we shift our thinking about egotistical to include how we often unconsciously let our ego shape our behavior—whether that means feeling superior or, conversely, less than?

When we let our ego drive us, we're being egotistical. And when we're being egotistical, it's less about a fixed character trait of self-absorption and more about a reactive state—one where the ego takes the lead and pulls us into patterns that might not serve us or those around us.

By recognizing that we all have egotistical moments or periods in life, we can begin to move out of reacting from a place of ego to responding with more awareness and balance as our higher selves.

Later in the book, I'll share more examples of how to harness the ego in healthy ways. But for the first bit, I'll be speaking more about the less-than-stellar aspects of the ego self.

You're about to read a story where I'm embarrassingly egotistical. Brandi felt the overwhelming need to impress Larissa—Adam's ex-girlfriend. This encounter unfolded when Larissa came to drop off the dog she and Adam had adopted a decade earlier. It's not a flattering story about me, but I share it with you because it perfectly illustrates some of my coping strategies from childhood that no longer serve me as an adult. As you read, it might just clue you in to a few of your own egotistical behaviors as well.

The Dog Drop-off

"Heads up," my husband's text reads. "Larissa is going to drop off Felix in twenty minutes."

Ignoring the sudden tension in my chest, I reply, "Sounds good!"

Felix was my husband Adam's adorable little mini-Aussie cuddle companion for eight years. When his relationship with Larissa ended, Felix stayed with her. Now, Adam only gets to cuddle Felix when his ex needs a dog sitter. And despite all the dog handoffs over the previous three years, I've only met Larissa once—briefly.

Adam and I are happily married—but being one year postpartum with our daughter, Vinni, I'm struggling physically, mentally, and emotionally. Between the exhaustion of motherhood at forty-three and still finding my footing after returning to work, I've been overwhelmed. I've tried to counteract the feeling of being a burden by portraying a sense of having my act together.

A dog drop-off is not a big deal, I repeat in my head as I notice the shift in my energy that feels a little bit like Bruce Banner transforming into the Incredible Hulk.

The thought of meeting my husband's ex-girlfriend with only twenty minutes' notice causes my stomach to drop and my shoulders to tense. Brandi is starting to take over, and I shift into reaction mode.

I enjoy Felix's sweet and cuddly company, too...so why am I feeling so anxious?

At the moment, I can't quite acknowledge that my anxious reaction likely stems from being up with the baby four times last night. I'm too tired to stop the train heading for a crash.

Since I can't seem to access any of my usual self-regulating skills, I put my teething baby on my hip, and Brandi starts cleaning the house like an ego on a mission.

I'd do this for anyone. Brandi tries to convince me that I'd quickly tidy up for any guest, though I know that's not true. Still, Brandi is on a roll, and at least the house is getting cleaned.

Fifteen minutes in, I look around and acknowledge that I've managed to pick up the toys, organize the catch-all pile, dust the shelves, vacuum the rug, straighten the shoes, and clear the kitchen counter. Everything within sight of the front door is now presentable in record time.

I take a deep breath in and slowly let it out for the first time in fifteen minutes.

I feel how tired I am.

On a "normal" day—whatever that even means anymore—a dog drop-off wouldn't be a big deal. But today, it feels like a punch to the gut. Why?

I take another on-purpose deep breath, a tool I've learned through both yoga and therapy. If I hadn't let Brandi take over, I'd probably still feel the tension, but I would be able to remind myself that I'm safe and loved and this is just a routine handoff, nothing more. I'd have noticed the stress without spiraling into cleaning mode to try and impress a stranger. I wouldn't have felt the need to pretend I wasn't exhausted and overwhelmed. But today, the deep breath is not enough, and my ego is still in charge.

Just as Brandi hypes me up to face the inevitable, another text from Adam comes through. "Larissa is running late. It'll be another hour before she drops off Felix."

Relief washes over me, and I collapse onto the couch with a deep exhale.

But the relief is fleeting, as Brandi quickly seizes the opportunity. *This is great! I have an hour to put the baby down for a nap, take a shower, do my makeup, put on actual non-yoga clothes, and sweep the front porch.*

It's wild to witness the low-self-esteem version of Brandi, who is very concerned about impressing everyone. And then, in an instant, she'll switch to the judgy version of ego that starts telling me how I *should* know better. *I should know better because I have spent so much time and energy becoming self-aware through therapy and yoga—I lead yoga teacher trainings for a living—why do I even care what anyone else thinks?*

I should know better. It runs on repeat in my mind as Brandi has me hurriedly put the baby down for a nap.

I shouldn't feel so anxious, as I frantically wash my hair and put makeup on.

I should be more calm, as Brandi has me ditch my standard athleisure mom uniform for jeans and a cute sweater.

I'm taking deep breaths, so I should be able to relax.

All the while, judgy Brandi is effectively *should-ing* all over me (pun intended). I feel helpless to the distinct urge to protect myself from an unwanted visitor by putting on the best show possible.

As soon as I see Larissa's car pull up, my anxiety spikes. *Should I just open the door and let the dog in?* That would be a healthy and appropriate choice. But no, that's not what I do. The sudden urge to make sure Larissa knows Adam is happy in his new life with his wife and kids is off the charts.

My higher self chimes into the conversation in my head. *I know Adam and Larissa have moved on—just as I've moved on from my previous relationship. There is nothing to prove here.*

Alas, no amount of higher consciousness logic can wrestle control back from my ego. It's like a fire alarm is going off in my head, and I'm running for the exit—which I don't realize is about to crescendo into one of the most cringe-worthy interactions I've ever had.

Brandi insists that I need to be holding my daughter when I answer the door. So, ignoring every rule about not waking a baby, I run downstairs to wake Vinni from her nap while simultaneously feeling appalled at my reactions.

When I open the door, I put on my best face that reads: *Here I am—calm, cool, and collected. I'm Adam's wife, and I'm holding our adorable baby.*

Felix is excited to be here and immediately runs into the house and onto his favorite spot on the back of the couch. There was a ton of snowfall the night before, so to make small talk, I say, "Crazy amount of snow last night—how were the roads coming back down the pass?"

Larissa says the roads were not bad at all and then generously offers, "Vinni is starting to look more like you than Adam."

At this, Brandi has a brilliant idea! I pull out my phone to show Larissa a baby picture of Adam that I happen to have handy, side by side with a picture of *our* baby at the same age.

Larissa raises her eyebrows and smiles. "They are practically twins!" Brandi feels both horrified at what she's doing and also satisfied.

But since the phone is already out, Brandi keeps scrolling through pictures of our beautiful, happy family for Larissa to see. Insert palm-to-forehead and slight nausea as I witness myself following Brandi's suggestion to hold the phone with my right hand and swipe through the pictures with my left hand—allowing my gorgeous wedding ring to catch the sunlight.

Thank the heavens, Larissa says she better get going.

As soon as the door closes, I exhale and hug my daughter to my chest.

Judgy Brandi chimes in, *You shouldn't have behaved that way. What were you thinking?*

But there's nothing I can do about it now. I close my eyes slowly and brace myself for the continued waves of shame I know are headed my way.

While it doesn't change what I felt in that moment, I find it makes sense that I felt the way I did. To understand why I reacted that way, let's start with a mini history lesson about the ego.

The Ego Throughout History

The concept of the ego self has been a central question across cultures around the world throughout human history. In Ancient Greece, philosophers like Plato and Aristotle grappled with the idea of the "self" and "soul." They sought to understand human nature and behavior, just as you will do through the practices I share in this book.

In yoga, the ego self—called ahamkara—is seen as both necessary and the source of suffering. It's something I constantly work on in my own practice, aiming to rise above its limitations and connect with my higher self. This dance between ego and higher self has been at the core of yogic philosophy for thousands of years.

In the early 1900s, Freud developed a model of the mind that includes the id, ego, and superego, which often mirror my own internal struggles, as you saw with Brandi in the last story. The id is like a wild child, seeking to feel good without caring about consequences. In Freud's model, the ego self tries to be more rational than the id— balancing the id's desires with the realities of the outside world. The superego (a.k.a. the judgy angel) acts as a moral compass based on society's rules and values. When Brandi takes the lead, I often feel caught in that conflict between impulse, control, and judgment.

In modern psychology, the ego plays a central role in understanding personality and behavior. When we understand how the ego self drives our thoughts and actions, we can make more mindful choices and develop healthier coping strategies.

In a very brief summary, the dance between the ego and higher self isn't a modern concept—it's something humans have been navigating for centuries. Whether it's ancient yogis striving to transcend the ego or Freud analyzing our inner workings, the challenges are universal. The tools and practices I share in this book are grounded in a rich history of ego philosophy. I hope they resonate with you and help you find more balance, self-awareness, and conscious action in your own life.

"There is no such thing as a new idea."
—MARK TWAIN

You might be like Brandi and find it difficult to face hard truths about yourself without spiraling into a circle of shame. Or you may be like others who seem to put blinders on and deny or defend their not-so-awesome reactive behaviors.

While it was a seemingly random idea from my friend, Mollie, it turns out that naming the ego self also points to several psychological techniques that I have since learned about. I'll briefly share my understanding of three of them.

1. IFS: Internal Family Systems Therapy (a.k.a "Parts Work")

Imagine your mind as a large house with many rooms, and in each room, a different part of your life—a happy part, a scared part, a brave part, and so on. Internal Family Systems (IFS) therapy is like walking through this house, exploring each room to understand the needs, feelings, and behaviors of each part. These parts represent different aspects of yourself, and sometimes, they may be in conflict. For example, the scared part might be hesitant to try new things, while the brave part wants to explore and take risks.

IFS therapy involves working with a therapist to actively engage with these different parts of yourself, helping you understand and address the underlying emotions driving anxiety, depression, or relationship difficulties. It's like having a conversation with each part, giving them a voice and a role in the healing process. The goal is not to suppress or ignore these parts, but to integrate them into a healthier, more harmonious self.

Naming my ego self as "Brandi" was a way of applying IFS principles in my own life. By giving my ego self a distinct identity, I could engage with it more consciously and compassionately. This naming created psychological distance, allowing me to recognize when Brandi was in control and giving me the opportunity to work with that part of myself rather than react from it. It allowed me to honor the role my ego self plays while also learning to integrate it in a way that supported my higher self and overall well-being.

2. Cognitive Defusion in Acceptance and Commitment Therapy (ACT)

Cognitive defusion is all about creating mental space between ourselves and our thoughts or emotions. Instead of getting caught up in what the ego is telling us, we can step back and see those thoughts for what they really are—just thoughts. In my case, when I'm able to see Brandi starting to react, cognitive defusion helps me pause and observe her without getting swept away in the emotions she stirs up. Note: I did not demonstrate this in the dog drop-off story.

When I'm grounded and feeling good physically, mentally, and emotionally, I can picture my thoughts like clouds drifting by in the sky. I don't have to cling to them, and I don't have to fight them either—I just let them float by. This practice allows me to detach from Brandi's judgments or defensiveness and take a more mindful approach. I can notice the thought—Brandi is feeling defensive right now—without letting it control my actions.

In ACT, cognitive defusion isn't about avoiding or pushing away uncomfortable thoughts. It's about acknowledging them and creating enough distance so they don't define how we respond. For example, if Brandi is anxious about a situation, instead of trying to suppress that anxiety, I'll note it: *I see your anxiety.* And I try not to let it take over. I stay connected to my higher self and what matters most in that moment.

The beauty of cognitive defusion is that it helps me see my thoughts more clearly, especially when Brandi is in charge. I can recognize the mental chatter and emotional triggers for what they are without overidentifying with them. This space allows me to act more in line with my values rather than reacting from a place of ego.

It's important to note that this process isn't about disconnecting from emotions or becoming numb. Instead, it's about finding balance. Often, cognitive defusion allows me to acknowledge Brandi's presence without letting her run the show. By creating this distance, there's more possibility of self-compassion and conscious choice, even when my ego wants to take over.

3. Illeism (pronounced i-lee-ism)

Studies by Ethan Kross, a psychologist at the University of Michigan, revealed that people who use third-person references during self-talk tend to handle stressful situations more effectively. He found that adopting a perspective where we address ourselves as separate entities can significantly alter our cognitive, emotional, and behavioral responses. This technique is called Illeism.

LeBron James (basketball player) and The Rock (Dwayne Johnson/wrestler/actor) may come to mind when you think about this. I assume they do it for publicity, with statements like, "LeBron James is a winner," and "The Rock doesn't need to be fixed; The Rock is perfect just the way he is."

Others may recognize the use of Illeism from Sesame Street or Seinfeld.

Elmo from Sesame Street says things like:
"Elmo's curious!"
"Elmo's ready for adventure!"
"Elmo's feeling silly!"

Jimmy from Seinfeld says things like:
"Jimmy thinks this is a bad idea."

"Jimmy's not happy about this."

"Jimmy's getting hungry."

"Jimmy's always up for a challenge."

While Elmo and Jimmy used Illeism for comedic effect, they demonstrate that with a little space/separation, it might feel easier to identify and talk about uncomfortable feelings and behaviors.

Your First Practice

The first interactive activity in this book will involve journaling. Before we dive in, I want to set the tone for what these journaling practices are all about. They are opportunities to pause and reflect. The hope is that you accept the invitation to engage with the material on a deeper level now. By putting pen to paper (or fingers and thumbs to keyboard), you'll be able to explore your thoughts, feelings, and experiences in a way that reading alone can't offer.

So, if you haven't already, take a moment to grab a notebook, open your journaling app, or use the <u>free companion workbook</u>. Find a quiet space where you can focus, and get ready to dive into some self-discovery.

These practices are designed to help you connect the ideas in the book to your own life, making the abstract more tangible and the journey more personal. There's no right or wrong way to do this—just start where you are and see what comes up.

Practice #1: Name Your Ego

For the purpose of the ego work we're doing in this book, we're combining Illeism (referring to oneself in the third person) with Internal Family Systems (IFS), also known as Parts Work. Then, by giving your ego self a name, you'll be able to create cognitive defusion.

The idea is to step back and observe ourselves from a more detached and objective perspective. This approach allows us to discuss and reflect on some of the more challenging aspects of our behavior and thoughts in a way that feels a bit lighter and less personal. By doing this, we can more easily recognize and admit how we're showing up in the world, which is the first step toward making meaningful changes.

Think of it as putting on a pair of glasses that lets you see yourself from the outside looking in. This little bit of distance can make all the difference in how we approach self-reflection and growth.

Over the years of sharing this practice, I've noticed that most people tend to give their ego self a name that starts with the same letter as their first name—but not always.

Sometimes it's a nickname people called you when you were a kid.

And other times it's completely random.

Without thinking too hard, what is your ego's name?

With a name for your ego, you can really dive in and have some discoveries and make changes.

A Practice for Tapping into Your Higher Self

Now that you've named your ego, it's time to identify and name your emotions so you can more easily tap back into your higher self. This brings me to Dr. Dan Siegel, a renowned psychiatrist and expert in the field of interpersonal neurobiology. His work is especially relevant here because he focuses on the mind-body connection and how our emotions affect our nervous system. He's widely known for his therapeutic work and for coining the phrase, "Name it to tame it." Dr. Siegel explains that when we name our emotions, we create space for our nervous system to relax, allowing those emotions to move through us, rather than staying stuck and creating more stress.

When I work with this concept of naming emotions, I think of the saying, "What you resist persists." In my experience, resistance to emotions often sounds like what you read in the dog drop-off story, where Brandi says things like, *I shouldn't be so mad*, or *I should have known better*.

I know it's my ego talking because the word "should" is involved. And if your ego self is anything like Brandi, it can easily turn one "should" into a spiral—what I like to call "circling the shame drain."

Returning momentarily to the dog drop-off story: After Larissa dropped off Felix and I closed the door, I circled the shame drain for a little while. To get myself out of the should-spiral, I used the following practice to acknowledge how I was feeling instead of resisting the emotions. It was the start of getting my higher self back in the driver's seat.

Practice #2: Acknowledge How You're Feeling

"Name it to Tame it" is a tool I've been using for years, even before I knew that Dr. Siegel was spreading the good news about it. By naming my emotions—I feel mad, I feel frustrated, I feel sad—I can take the reins back from Brandi and tap into my higher self. This practice helps me create space for those emotions to flow through, rather than letting them continue to control me.

In your journal or in your head:

1. **Take a deep breath in and out and check in with yourself physically.**

   Fill in the blank with one or two words. "Right now, physically, I feel..." (relaxed, tired, tense, tight, soft, etc.).

2. **Take another deep breath in and out and check in with yourself mentally and emotionally.**

   Fill in the blank with one or two words. "Right now, mentally and emotionally, I feel..." (open, anxious, sad, happy, brave, afraid, silly, etc.).

Notice if there is any resistance to how you're feeling. If you feel tired, but also mad about feeling tired, notice that, and we will circle back to that in the next chapter.

The first step on this journey of self-discovery involves recognizing when your ego self is taking the lead. This does not mean we're working to eliminate the ego self—after all, it serves important functions related to our survival and identity. Instead, it's about seeing it first. From there, you will learn how to balance it and allow the higher self to guide your thoughts, actions, and decisions.

Action Steps

At the end of each chapter, you'll find a summary of the key practices we've discussed, called Action Steps. These are your reminders to integrate what you've learned by consistently engaging with these practices. By doing so, you'll be able to deepen your understanding and experience the full benefits of the ego work we're doing together. So, as you move through the book, make it a point to revisit these Action Steps and actively incorporate them into your daily life.

Action Steps for Chapter 1

This is your invitation to get present with yourself in a new way. Having named your ego, you'll find it easier to recognize when you're being egotistical. Additionally, acknowledging how you're feeling throughout your day is a simple yet powerful step in becoming more present, allowing your higher self to take the lead.

- Practice #1: Name Your Ego
- Practice #2: Acknowledge How You're Feeling

In Summary

Naming the ego self helps create a sense of distance, allowing us to recognize unhealthy or unhelpful reactive habits more clearly. While we often associate being "egotistical" with arrogance, it can just as easily manifest as shame or a constant need to prove ourselves. In this chapter, I introduced the concept of the ego self across different historical contexts, explored parallels in therapeutic techniques for working with the ego, and presented the "Name it to Tame It" tool as a way to bring awareness to our physical, mental, and emotional states in any given moment.

Moving Forward

In the next chapter, we will explore more tools and practices to help you identify and understand your ego self. More importantly, you will learn how to cultivate a stronger connection with your higher self, allowing it to guide you toward a more fulfilling and authentic life.

CHAPTER 2

Dear Ego Self

Now that you have a general understanding of what the ego self is and that we all have one, I invite you to zoom in a bit and start getting to know how your ego developed and how it's trying to help you. If we learn to recognize, understand, and even appreciate this part of ourselves, it can become a source of insight and growth and feel like a blessing. However, if we remain unaware of how it influences our behavior, it can create unnecessary conflict and cause us to self-sabotage. It could feel like a curse.

A Blessing and a Curse

For as long as I can remember, I've had a knack for walking into a room full of people and immediately sensing the unspoken—like reading the subtle shifts in energy or picking up on the quiet undertones of emotion. It's as if the room itself whispers to me what everyone is feeling and needing. As a business owner, this intuitive ability became a gift, allowing me to nurture and grow a community of yogis who felt seen and understood.

The ironic part? During the first eight years of building that community, while I could tune into everyone else, I remained blind to my own inner landscape. I had no idea what I was feeling or needing, lost in the current of trying to meet everyone else's expectations.

From an early age, I learned that if I could keep everyone else happy, maybe—just maybe—conflict could be avoided, and I wouldn't have to face the pain of abandonment. This coping mechanism, that I now know as hypervigilance, is like living with radar always on, constantly scanning for threats, predicting others' needs to keep the peace and maintain a sense of safety.

What I once thought of as a kind of psychic gift for reading people, I now see was a survival strategy—a reactive pattern that was necessary in childhood but is no longer necessary as an adult. I see it's the reason I stayed in an unhealthy relationship for sixteen years.

I met Derek in 2004, when I was twenty-four. It was a perfect example of a codependent relationship. To be liked, let alone loved, by him felt extremely special—like I was chosen. He built me tangible things— like a straw bale house and a car that ran on waste vegetable oil. He built out the interior of my yoga studio. But in return, I unconsciously shrank and hid my emotional needs.

There didn't seem to be room for both of us to have them, so I let his emotions and needs take precedence. This dynamic seemed perfectly normal to me because shrinking and hiding had been my ego's way of navigating the world since childhood.

Fast-forward to 2019, when we were married with a two-and-a-half-year-old son. I was approaching forty and stewarding a vibrant yoga community in Colorado. Despite all the outward success, I didn't yet understand the dynamics between my ego self and my higher self.

When I was teaching yoga and with my friends, I generally operated from my higher self, Brittany. But in my marriage, I'm sad to admit, Brandi often took the lead, reacting out of old wounds and survival strategies.

Looking back, I can see it was both a blessing and a curse that, at the start of our sixteenth year together, a repressed traumatic memory from my childhood resurfaced. The details aren't relevant here, but remembering them at age thirty-nine was a significant wake-up call that ultimately led to major growth and changes in how I operated.

Suddenly, everything I thought I knew about myself and my history felt like a game of fifty-two-card pick-up—scattered and chaotic. Some pieces of my past landed face up, others face down, and it all felt like a mess I needed to sort through. The only thing that was clear was I knew I needed to show up healthier for myself, my son, and everyone around me. So I began working with a therapist and a coach.

The therapist taught me about boundary setting—which I had done very little of in my life. While this was good in theory, I was finding it hard to address the self-sabotaging behaviors I brought to the relationship—behaviors that needed to change if I truly wanted to show up healthy and authentically.

Introducing Brandi's Reactive Strategies:

Before we move forward, I want to take a moment to zoom in on something that's been a core part of my journey with my ego self. Often, when we think of someone "reacting," we imagine outbursts of anger or overt conflict. But reactions can take on many forms, some of which are much more subtle and harder to recognize. For me, Brandi developed a set of survival strategies that weren't about yelling or confrontation at all. Instead, they were more about retreating and accommodating.

Take, for example, a situation when I was working at a college prep boarding school and was asked to take on yet another project, even though my plate was already full. Brandi would shrink, minimizing what I felt, wanted, and needed. She didn't want to stir the pot, so she'd agree to take on the extra work, even though it added more stress. Brandi would freeze in response to the conflict between wanting to say no but fearing disappointing others, pushing me to work harder and overextend myself in pursuit of being valued for what I accomplished.

Today, now that I know how to lead from my higher self, I would approach the situation differently. I would pause, assess my current workload, and calmly assert that while I value the opportunity, I simply don't have the bandwidth to take on more right now. I would speak from a place of self-awareness and clarity, recognizing that boundaries are essential for my well-being and productivity.

In personal relationships, let's say there's a disagreement at home. Brandi would freeze, avoiding the conflict altogether, and then fawn, trying to please the other person to restore harmony—even at the cost of my own emotional needs. She would put on a smile and try to smooth things over to avoid rocking the boat, even if it meant my feelings went unacknowledged.

But my higher self would navigate the conflict with more confidence. I would express my feelings openly, without retreating into people-pleasing mode. I would understand that it's okay to have uncomfortable conversations and that expressing my needs doesn't threaten the relationship—it strengthens it.

I'm not proud of Brandi's reactive ego strategies, but I can see why they made sense when I was a kid. They were my ways of coping with conflict and trying to protect myself. But as I grow, I'm learning to let my higher self take the lead more often, shifting from reactivity to conscious action.

After six months of processing the repressed childhood memory in therapy, I could see how it made sense that I stayed in the relationship with Derek for so long.

While it didn't make the hard things easy, per se, no longer letting Brandi unconsciously take the lead made stepping out of denial and into acceptance and action less difficult.

A New Way Forward: Action Instead of Reaction

It was at this time that I had the phone conversation with Mollie where Brandi was named. I began to take action and let my higher self, Brittany, lead the way in my life more often.

I recognized what was needed for me to continue healing, and I also realized what I wanted to model as a healthy relationship for our son. So, I requested some necessary changes from Derek, hoping that we could grow healthier together. I understood how it might seem unfair to him, after so many years of operating a certain way, to suddenly shift the dynamic. But it also wasn't fair to my higher self to keep living by old, unspoken standards that no longer served me, or us.

Under the old terms of the relationship, Derek hadn't physically abandoned me, which was all Brandi cared about. She was terrified to let my higher self take the lead, fearing that asking for changes might mean he'd leave. Brandi doubted whether I was worth it to him, convinced that the marriage was easier for him when I stayed in her mode—quiet, accommodating, minimizing my emotional needs. She tried to pull me back, urging me to turn the car around and return to how things were, where she could stay "safe."

But from my higher self's perspective, I could see that what mattered most was honoring what I needed emotionally in the relationship.

Holding those boundaries was one of the hardest things I had ever done. It felt like flexing muscles I didn't even know I had. With every conversation, there were emotional growing pains—my inner resistance, Brandi's fear of abandonment, and the struggle to keep choosing myself and a healthy relationship over my old habits.

Instead of letting Brandi take the lead, I found myself constantly reassuring her: *He may abandon this relationship, but I will not abandon myself anymore.*

Even as I tried to calm her down, reminding her that I was worthy, capable, and strong—that I would be okay no matter what happened—the fears still burned inside me. I knew I needed a way to tame those fears, to quiet the noise, and that's when I became serious with my practice of meditation.

Meditation became a lifeline for me during that transformative period, complementing the support I was receiving from therapy. To understand why meditation helped settle my restless ego mind, picture these two scenarios:

Scenario #1: A person is guiding an elephant through a busy marketplace. It's chaos—the elephant's trunk is constantly wandering, knocking over stalls, grabbing at fruit, and causing mayhem.

Scenario #2: Now imagine the same person handing the elephant a stick of bamboo to hold in its trunk. With the trunk occupied, the elephant walks calmly through the marketplace, leaving everything undisturbed.

Our ego thoughts are like that wandering trunk, constantly reaching for distractions and causing internal chaos. Sometimes, to keep the ego self in check, we need to give it something to focus on—

something like an affirmation or a Sanskrit mantra—to help anchor us and prevent those distractions from taking over.

I bring this up because, up to that point in my adult life, I had an on-again, off-again relationship with meditation, especially with body scan techniques where you mentally focus on and relax each part of your body from head to toe. During this time, Mollie invited me to try a twenty-one-day Sanskrit mantra-based meditation practice, committing to thirty minutes of silent meditation each day.

The mantra I used was "So Hum," a simple yet powerful phrase that became the metaphorical stick of bamboo I handed Brandi during my meditations.

"So Hum" translates from Sanskrit to "I am." Some interpret it as "I am that" or even "I am that I am." With each inhalation, I would mentally say, "So," and with each exhalation, "Hum." This mantra can be understood in various spiritual and philosophical contexts, symbolizing the connection between the individual self and the greater universal consciousness. By repeating this mantra, I found that Brandi's distractions and anxieties had less room to roam. It gave her something to hold on to, allowing me to stay grounded and present in the moment.

Great, but Brandi hates meditation.

At first, Brandi repeatedly set down the bamboo stick—the mantra— and I had to keep asking her to pick it back up. Every time I tried to focus, she would throw it down like a stubborn child. Sometimes it felt like she was kicking and screaming inside my head, refusing to stay still, listing out all the things from my to-do list I *should* be doing instead: *There are emails to answer and laundry to fold!*

On other days, Brandi's resistance was more like a sulky teenager slouched in the back of the room, arms crossed. She would let me sit on the cushion while she muttered things like, *This is a waste of time.* My body would itch to get up, and my mind would race, trying to convince me that staying seated wasn't worth the effort. And still, I stayed.

Brandi's resistance in meditation often reminded me of my son having a meltdown. Trying to reason with him in the moment was pointless—there's no talking sense into a dysregulated nervous system. Instead, I let him know I was there, breathed deeply, and held space for his big feelings until he eventually softened and crawled into my lap for comfort. In much the same way, I've learned to hold space for Brandi during meditation. Instead of fighting her or trying to force her to calm down, I simply sit with her reactions. I've come to see her resistance as a mirror, reflecting parts of myself I don't usually have time to notice in the busyness of day-to-day life.

And when she finally settles into the routine—usually ten to fifteen minutes into the practice—I feel the peace people often talk about experiencing in meditation. It's wonderful. There's more space between the thoughts, and the grip of the mantra softens. Eventually, even the mantra itself melts away, leaving me in a stillness I don't often find anywhere else.

It's hard work, but it's healing work.

A lot of healing took place during those early thirty-minute meditation practices. As I sat in stillness, I held space for Brandi and all the pain and survival strategies she had carried since my early years. But I also held space for forty-year-old Brittany, who was coming to terms with the reality that her relationship with Derek—the relationship that had defined ages twenty-four through forty—was not going to change in the way she had hoped. It was likely ending.

Meditation was a lifeline, and with the world shutting down for the 2020 pandemic barely six months later, there couldn't have been a better time to deepen that practice.

Amidst the COVID lockdown, meditation helped keep my sanity in check. Of course, there were still times when Brandi threw tantrums—when she would resist sitting in stillness, restless and frustrated—but the more I practiced, the easier it became to soothe her. Over time, I learned that taming my ego wasn't about suppressing it; it was about acknowledging it and creating space for its reactions without letting them take over.

It's a practice, not a perfect.

In addition to my consistent meditation practice, I began intentionally checking in with myself throughout the day. I started asking, *How am I feeling physically right now? How am I feeling mentally and emotionally? And is Brandi taking the lead?*

This practice of self-inquiry allowed me to act as my higher self more consistently—in my relationship and in life. There were still times when Brandi would whisper her doubts: *This is too hard. Why bother? You'll never change.* But I came to realize that Brandi's voice was just an echo of old patterns and fears, trying to keep me safe in ways that no longer served me. It reminded me of something my yoga teacher, Baron Baptiste, said often, "You have thoughts, but you are not your thoughts—and they definitely don't have to run the show."

What kept me going was the understanding that every small step, every moment of awareness, was a victory. I reminded myself that this was a practice—and life was never going to be perfect. I embraced the idea that growth happens in the discomfort, in those moments when we choose to act differently, even when it's challenging.

I was, and still am, far from perfect. Moment by moment, I committed to staying in the discomfort of honoring my needs—for myself, the relationship, and what I wanted our son to witness as healthy love. But it wasn't easy. There were many moments where Brandi tried to pull me back, urging me to compromise my boundaries for the sake of keeping the peace. She would whisper things like, *Isn't it easier to just stay quiet?* Or, *What if this all falls apart?* She feared the unknown and clung to the familiar patterns, even if they no longer served me.

In the past, I would have backtracked or softened my requests, letting Brandi take over to avoid the discomfort. But this time, I stayed with it, honoring my truth, even as Brandi's fears bubbled up.

As these hard conversations became more frequent, it became clear that Derek wasn't going to meet me in the changes I was asking for. I recognized that staying true to my needs was more important than clinging to a version of the relationship that wasn't healthy for either of us.

Each request for change—whether it was about emotional connection, shared responsibilities, or communication—was met with resistance, not just from Derek, but from Brandi as well. But Brittany continued to hold the line, insisting that the relationship evolve into something healthier or not continue at all. The more I honored my needs, the clearer it became that our paths were diverging.

Ultimately, in the spring of 2020, the marriage ended. It wasn't a sudden decision, but the culmination of many moments where Brittany stood firm while Brandi wrestled with the fear of abandonment. I realized that honoring my higher self, and showing my son what healthy love looks like, meant letting go of the relationship. It was one of the hardest decisions I've ever made, but I knew it was the right one.

Naming Brandi Changed Everything

When Mollie introduced me to the idea of naming my ego self back in 2019, it changed how I experience life. Naming Brandi gave me a way to recognize when my ego was leading, and it allowed me to consciously choose a different path. This simple practice has helped me step out of unconscious habits and into a more intentional way of living, positively impacting every area of my life.

If I could make these changes that far into life, I'm confident you can, too. The key is being willing to be vulnerable and commit to seeing and speaking to this part of yourself in new, more compassionate ways.

How Meditation Can Help

I'd say 90 percent of the people I work with think they can't meditate because they can't stop their minds from thinking. There's good news and bad news about this concern.

I'll start with the bad news: You will never stop your thoughts. Thoughts are a part of the human experience.

The good news is: Your thoughts are your primary source for clues about your ego.

Meditation is many things, but it's not the practice of stopping thinking. It's a practice of remembering. I don't mean remembering things about your life or to-do list. I mean remembering who you are without all the added baggage your ego self has piled on.

Think about a baby. They're just a lump discovering what's possible in their body. They're learning to move the things on their body that we have labeled hands, feet, eyes, etc. It looks like an exploration of what happens if they try something. Yes, there seem to be deep preferences for comfort, connection, and nourishment. But there doesn't seem to be a self-doubt about whether their actions are good, bad, or otherwise.

In meditation, you practice giving your mind a simple task, so that the ego can let go for a moment or more, and you can remember who you are without all the judgments.

Remember the elephant and bamboo stick metaphor? In meditation, you give your ego a task. In this style of meditation, the task is to focus on the mantra, so your nervous system can have a little break.

Some days, Brandi is so squirrelly that she refuses a mantra. This next practice is a nice alternative to a mantra meditation. In the guided meditation, I give you something to "think" about while sitting still and show you how to meditate without your ego running amok.

Practice #3: I'm Breathing in, and I'm Breathing out Meditation

You can practice this independently after reading through the exercise. I also have a recorded version on my website at: www.brittanyhopkins.com/breathing.

1. **Setup:**

Sit on a chair with a pillow behind your lower back, so your spine is straight, your chest can be open, and your shoulders relaxed.

2. **Set a Timer:**

Set it for at least five minutes.

3. **Physical Check-In:**

Without judgment, notice any tight or tense places in your body.

4. **Mental and Emotional Check-In:**

Without judgment, name how you're feeling (e.g., happy, sad, clear, cloudy, etc.).

5. **Focus on Breath:**

For the remainder of the time, give your mind the task of following your breath.
   - As you breathe in, say to yourself, "I'm breathing in."
   - As you breathe out, say to yourself, "I'm breathing out."

6. **Closing Check-In:**

Once the timer goes off, put one hand on top of the other against your sternum:
   - Without judgment, notice how your body is feeling now.
   - Without judgment, name how you're feeling mentally and emotionally now.

Different Options for Finishing Your Meditation:

→ **Offer gratitude** to yourself for committing to the practice.

→ **Say any blessing** you like silently or aloud. This is my favorite: "May all beings everywhere be blessed with happiness and freedom. May the thoughts, words, and actions of my own life contribute to that happiness and freedom for all."

(Sanskrit Translation: Lokah Samastah Sukhino Bhavantu)

→ **Set an intention** to carry the calm or clarity from your meditation into the rest of your day.

After your meditation, take a few moments to reflect on the experience. Did you notice any shifts in your physical, mental, or emotional state? It's helpful to remember that meditation is not about achieving a specific outcome, but about observing and accepting what is present in the moment.

You could consider keeping a meditation journal where you briefly note how you felt before and after your practice. Over time, this can become a powerful tool for noticing patterns, shifts, and areas of growth.

Knowing it Worked

How will you know if your meditation practice is working? It might not be immediately obvious, but over time, you may notice subtle changes in how you respond to challenges, how you relate to yourself and others, and how you experience your thoughts and emotions. Meditation is about the gradual cultivation of mindfulness and presence, and the benefits often manifest in moments when you realize you're reacting less, feeling more grounded, or simply carrying a greater sense of peace in your day-to-day life.

There will be times that meditation might be like eating vegetables to stay healthy. Sometimes, the veggies are yummy, and sometimes, they're not. It doesn't matter if they're yummy or not. What matters is that you eat them because they're necessary for your health. Similarly, what matters in meditation is the consistency of your practice, not whether each session feels perfect.

Over time, you will see progress. Remember to have compassion for yourself as you continue on this journey.

It's not magic; it's just practice.

With consistent practice, I have had all sorts of meditation experiences that Brandi has labeled good, bad, peaceful, frustrating, etc. There are times that I feel anxious or sad during meditation. There have been times that thoughts or memories surface that I've needed to work through with my therapist. And there are times that I feel peaceful and happy. In reality, the hundreds of hours of meditation practices over the last five years don't actually need to be labeled anything other than practices. Nothing more or less.

Regardless of how I've felt during any one meditation practice, every moment of meditation has brought me closer to my true self.

Take it one breath at a time.

A Letter to Your Ego Self

I'm very excited to share this next practice, which requires a bit of a time commitment but provides a *huge* return.

The practice is to write a letter to your ego self. This is helpful because instead of resisting the ego, it's an opportunity to have compassion for that part of yourself. It creates space to allow and understand that your ego has done a lot to support you and keep you safe throughout your life.

Many authors and teachers include this in their work. The formula for the letter to your ego self that I use came from Terry Real, a therapist and creator of Relational Life Therapy. In his work, he uses the terms Adaptive Child and Reactive Strategies for the part of ourselves that we default to letting run the show in conflict, or times of stress.

Practice #4: Letter to Your Ego Self

In a journal, you can try out the following formula:

1. **Dear [ego self name],**
2. **Thank you for...**
3. **What you've given me...**
4. **What you've cost me...**
5. **The plan moving forward...**

Sample Letter

Here is a sample letter from one of my students. It's pretty standard in many ways, so feel free to copy parts that resonate and add or delete from other parts.

Dear Stu,

Thank you for all that you've done for me to keep me as safe as possible. Especially as a kid, being raised in a family where, while your parents were doing the best they could with the cards they were dealt, you were not seen, heard, understood, or protected in many ways. I needed you to adapt and shape-shift when Dad was around. He was the family's breadwinner, so to be fed/clothed/housed, you needed to do your best not to rock the boat. Part of that meant staying small, being really good, and being well behaved. Even though you weren't sure how to manage your big feelings in your tiny body, you figured it out. Your dad was an alcoholic, and you needed to be hypervigilant and know how he was feeling and if he had been drinking, to stay out of his line of fire.

Then there was your mom, who didn't have the ability to tap into her own emotional needs in healthy ways, let alone anyone else's. She was so far walled off and disconnected from herself that you didn't have access to all the emotional support you needed. So you set out to get love from her. What you figured out to do was to get straight A's, work your butt off at basketball, and any other achievement you could get your hands on. Because when you did those things, you got the attention you craved from her.

So it makes sense that you learned to shape-shift to be safe and achieve things to be loved. As sad as it is, you did a really good job figuring out how to adapt as a small person to stay safe and get love!

You've given me an unbelievable work ethic, the ability to read people, make them comfortable, and make them feel that they matter, the strength and resilience to step up to the plate over and over again, and so many life accomplishments that I'm very proud of.

I needed all of those coping skills to survive the family dynamics as a child. But as an adult, **what you have cost me** is a sense of my value and worth—separate from how others see me. You have cost me the ability to trust myself to stand up or speak up, as soon as I question someone else's judgments/actions. You've cost me time being fully present with myself and my children because you spend so much time worrying if others will leave you. You've cost me health because of a lifetime's worth of hypervigilance and anxiety trying to make sure everyone else is okay/taken care of while my body has been overcompensating and suffering.

Stu, I need you to know that I see you, and I hear your desperate desire to matter and be cared for in the ways that your parents weren't able to care for you. It makes total sense that you adapted to survive as you did. It also makes sense that I regress to your coping techniques regularly, especially when I'm tired physically, mentally, and emotionally from the day-to-day needs of working and living.

There's a BIG BUT here. I'm intelligent, strong, funny, handsome, loving, and a very capable adult now. And I've got us. **Here's the plan moving forward.** Anytime you need a moment to be seen, heard, and understood, you can tug on my shirt sleeve and say, "Excuse me, Stanley, I need you for a minute." And as soon as humanly possible, I can step into another room and reassure you and remind you of whatever you need. It may sound like, "Sarah seems distant after she got home. It makes sense that you are hypervigilant and default to figuring out what is going on with her. You are afraid that you are going to be abandoned. AND we're okay. I'm a kind and loving human with all the skills to care for us. While all sorts of things could happen in life, I've got us."

Or, "You feel like you don't matter because you are not as good at that thing that someone else seems to be better at. It makes sense that you feel that way because that was demonstrated to you as a child. You primarily got attention and love when you succeeded."

I need you to hear me when I say that we do matter. We are already really good at some things and getting better at the other things we work on every day, and everything is good and getting better.

This is an important one, so listen to me. You are safe. There is nothing anyone can do to take our power away. You may accidentally give it away, but I can get it back instantly if you do give it away. I will also be our spokesperson and speak up whenever there is a need to speak up.

I know it will take some practice and time for you to trust me because I've let you run the show for too long. But I promise that you can trust me. I'm strong and capable, loving, and kind. I've got us!

Yours truly,
Stanley

What to do After Writing Your Letter

Writing this letter can be a powerful and emotional experience. After you finish, there are a few things you could do next:

→ **Read it Aloud:** Find a quiet spot and read your letter out loud to yourself. Hearing your voice say the words helps you connect with what you've written and gives you a sense of acknowledgment and release.

→ **Reflect and Revisit:** Keep your letter somewhere safe, like in your journal, so that you can look back on it later. It's a great way to see how you're growing and strengthening your relationship with your ego self.

→ **Burn or Destroy the Letter:** After reading the letter aloud, if it feels right, you might want to burn it or tear it up as a symbolic way of letting go of the past and moving forward.

→ **Share with a Trusted Person:** Consider sharing your letter with a close friend or therapist if you're comfortable. Talking it out with someone else can provide extra support and clarity.

→ **Take some time for self-care.** Whether going for a walk, meditating, or doing some gentle yoga—anything that grounds you is a good idea.

Remember, this whole process is about discovering more about yourself so you can step out of reaction in your life and into action, so remember to take care of yourself along the way.

Take a deep breath in.

Pause.

Like you're blowing through a straw, breathe out.

It Makes Sense That You Feel That Way

Now that you understand both the gifts and costs of your ego, and how you want to support it moving forward, you may still notice resistance in your daily life—just as I do with Brandi. This often happens when we experience any emotions other than happiness.

It's likely because, as a child, you weren't always encouraged to feel or express the full range of your emotions, a contrast to how things are today.

An Example of How Times Are Changing with Feelings:

One day, I was driving my deeply feeling five-year-old to school. We were both quiet, still recovering from his big emotions about getting out the door for school. After a bit of driving and breathing, I told him, "Even though it's hard sometimes, I'm grateful that you feel safe to share your big feelings with me."

He paused for a suspicious ten seconds and then, incredulously, asked, "Why?!"

I explained, "Well, when I was a kid, grown-ups typically said things like, 'Stop crying,' 'You're fine,' or 'You're okay.'"

His response makes me giggle every time I think about it: "You mean people in the '80s didn't feel their feelings?!"

Back in the present, Brandi often shows up with resistance, thinking or acting like she shouldn't feel all of the feelings. But now, because I understand why she feels certain things, I can do the next practice and say things like:

It makes sense that you feel mad. It makes sense that you feel frustrated. It makes sense that you feel sad.

When I do that, it seems to loosen Brandi's energetic grip. It shifts into a reparenting moment for me, where I'm comforting little Brittany, who became Brandi, and giving her permission to move through her feelings rather than resist or deny them.

Practice #5: It Makes Sense That You Feel...

As you continue to build a healthier relationship with your ego self, it's important to practice acknowledging your feelings in the moment, rather than resisting them. This next exercise is an expansion of the Name it to Tame it Practice in Chapter 1. It's designed to help you give yourself permission to feel whatever you're feeling as it comes up.

In your journal/workbook:

1. **Take a deep breath in and out, and check in with yourself physically.**

   Fill in the blank with one or two words. "Right now, physically, I feel _____" (relaxed, tired, tense, tight, soft, etc.).

   Then, notice if you feel any resistance to your feelings. If there is resistance, fill in the blank. "It makes sense that you feel _____ because _____."

   Example: It makes sense that you feel tired because you have been working extra hard on the project at work.

2. **Take another deep breath in and out and check in with yourself mentally and emotionally.**

   Fill in the blank with one or two words. "Right now, mentally and emotionally, I feel _____" (open, anxious, sad, happy, brave, afraid, silly, etc.).

   Then notice if there is any resistance to how you're feeling. If there is resistance then fill in the blanks. "It makes sense that you feel _____ because _____."

Example #1: It makes sense that you feel overwhelmed because being a parent and a full-time employee is a lot.

Example #2: It makes sense that you feel anxious about your partner being distant when they get home from work. Your habit of keeping us safe is to depend on other people for your well-being, and if they're distant, your warning sirens go off. But I've got us. They can be however they need to be. If I need to request a change of behavior, I'm capable of doing that. But if they're simply tired and need some space to land after work, we can give them that without feeling like the world is going to end.

Once you've finished the practice, take a moment to:

→ **Pause and Breathe:** After journaling, take a few deep breaths and give yourself time to simply be with whatever feelings came up. Sometimes, just sitting with your emotions without judgment can be incredibly grounding.

→ **Integrate Your Insights:** Reflect on what you've learned from this practice. How could you carry this awareness with you throughout your day? Set timers in your phone with labels to remind you to check in with yourself and offer, "It makes sense that you feel..." This can empower you to navigate challenging emotions with grace and control.

→ **Practice Self-Compassion:** If you uncover any resistance or challenging feelings, remember to offer yourself some kindness. Place a hand on your chest and say something like, "I'm doing my best, and it's okay to feel this way."

→ **Move Your Body:** Sometimes, emotions feel stuck in the body, so consider going for a walk or doing some gentle stretching. Gentle stretching can help release any tension or stress that might have come up during the practice, improving your physical and emotional well-being. I have a few practices you can use for free on my website, www. brittanyhopkins.com/move.

→ **Revisit:** Over time, you might notice patterns in how you respond to certain feelings. This can be a powerful tool to deepen your self-awareness and continue to build a healthier relationship with your ego self. Stay committed to this journey of self-improvement.

Simply notice and begin again.

Like many things in life, these are practices that I do repeatedly. Sometimes it's once a week. Sometimes it's every day. If you've let your ego run the show of your life as long as I have let Brandi, then it will take some time to make the shifts. And to be honest, Brandi takes the lead more often if I'm tired and overwhelmed.

I've struggled through it and found balance through it all. I believe you can find your way, too.

Action Steps for Chapter 2

The Action Steps for this chapter are here to help you deepen your understanding of your ego self and strengthen your connection with your higher self. The key is to engage with these practices consistently, allowing them to integrate naturally into your daily life.

- Practice #3: I'm Breathing In, and I'm Breathing Out Meditation
- Practice #4: Write a Letter to Your Ego Self
- Practice #5: It Makes Sense That You Feel...

By taking your time with these steps, you'll start to manage your ego self more easily and take the lead as your higher self more quickly.

In Summary

Writing the letter to Brandi and recognizing how she influences my thoughts and actions was a transformative step. Then letting myself know that it makes sense that I feel however I'm feeling in a moment has allowed me to start seeing my behaviors from a place of compassion rather than judgment. This journey has taught me that understanding and accepting the ego self is the first step toward true personal growth.

Life will always have its highs and lows, its ups and downs. However, with practice, you'll find that the lows become less daunting and the highs more fulfilling. The more you understand and accept your ego self, the more empowered you become to let your higher self take the lead in your life, making conscious, purposeful choices every day with little flourishes from your ego giving yourself character.

Moving Forward

In the next chapter, we will dive deeper into the intricate dance between your ego and higher self. You'll learn to identify the often hidden yet impactful messages your ego tells you, and how to challenge and transform the messages into empowered statements. This awareness is crucial in shifting from a reactive state to one of mindful action, where you can fully embrace your true potential.

Remember, the journey of self-discovery and growth is ongoing. It's not about achieving perfection, but about making continuous, conscious efforts to live authentically and compassionately.

With each step, each practice, and each breath, you will move closer to embodying the person you want to be. Let's continue this journey together, one chapter at a time.

CHAPTER 3

It's Mostly Lies

I'm really excited to tell you about the lies that Brandi tells me all the time, but first, let's take a moment to reflect on your experience so far:

What name did you give your ego?

How is it going naming your feelings? When you name your feelings, are you also offering yourself the grace of saying, "It makes sense that I feel that way"?

Have you tried meditation to quiet your ego self and calm your nervous system?

How did it feel to write the letter to your ego? Was it easy? Was it hard? Did you cry? Brandi really wants to know if it was hard and if you cried. She's a bit nosey that way and wants the juicy details.

Remember, this book is meant to both challenge and support you. The more you start uncovering these feelings and naming your reactive side, you will notice a pattern. Many of the thoughts that trigger your reactive self are mostly lies.

In this chapter, I'll be sharing about the limiting beliefs—the lies—that our ego uses when it's trying to take the lead in our lives. I'll tell a story about the limiting belief Brandi has held about me as a dancer for most of my life, and how it shaped so much of how I've seen myself and the world around me. My limiting beliefs have held me back in ways I didn't even realize until I was thirty-three. I'll take you on a journey back in time to uncover the origins of your own limiting beliefs and see how they tend to show up for you as an adult as unconscious ego statements. From there, you'll discover a new way of letting your higher self take the lead by creating empowered statements.

But first, let me tell you about the lies Brandi still tries to tell me daily, that were formed during my time as a young dancer.

Tiny Dancer

I was six years old, sitting in the audience in my little yellow daisy tutu, my legs swinging off the edge of the chair as I waited for my turn to perform. The stage lights flickered, casting long shadows, and I could feel the excitement buzzing in the room as the big kids danced. My mom, watching me from the side, told me years later that she saw my eyes light up in that moment.

The previous year of dance lessons had been a battle—I tried to quit about every other week—but on this particular day, watching the older girls twirl and leap with grace at the end-of-year recital, something shifted inside me. In an instant, the magic of dance clicked, and I was hooked. Little Brittany practically said, "Sign me up for another year—or the rest of my life. I'm in love!"

As the years passed, my love for dance grew, and I developed a work ethic to match it. By the time I was twelve, my parents were driving me an hour each way, five days a week, to a larger studio that competed in dance competitions. I made the list for a "dance company," and I was bursting with pride.

What happened next is blurry, like a half-remembered dream. Whether or not it happened exactly as I recall, it shaped me nonetheless.

The dance studio lobby was often a chaotic place, buzzing with the sounds of parents chatting, kids rushing in and out of classes, and the constant shuffle of dance bags across the floor. I remember standing in that crowded lobby, waiting for my class to start. Through a window, I could see into one of the dance rooms. I overheard one of the dance teachers say, "It's really sweet how much she loves to dance. Too bad she'll never go anywhere with it."

It felt like a punch to my stomach.

The words sank into me, cold and sharp, and made themselves at home. I was in seventh grade, an awkward age when everything feels amplified—emotions, insecurities, fears. I was tall and lanky, and people would jokingly call me a bean pole with a butt. I tried to convince myself that the teachers placed me in the back of the group because of my height, but after overhearing that comment, the reality seemed clear: I wasn't good enough to be in the front.

That seed was planted deep inside me, a tiny voice whispering, "You're not good enough." From that moment, I spent much of my life reacting unconsciously to that belief, letting it steer my decisions, my self-worth, and how I showed up in the world. It was no longer a comment made in passing—it had become a story I carried with me into adulthood.

But it didn't feel like a story about me. It felt like a fact.

How to be "Good Enough"

Also around this time, I noticed my mom had a gift for making beautiful flower arrangements. I asked her why she was so good at it, and I wasn't. She smiled and said, "Because I've been practicing a long time."

That was a moment of clarity for me: *If I'm not good enough at something, I just need to work harder. Then I will be good enough.*

What she said was a valuable lesson, one I want my own kids to understand: *If you want to be good at something, you may need to work hard to get it.* But the difference, which my mom couldn't have known, was that I unconsciously internalized this lesson in reaction to the story my little ego self had made up after hearing what my dance teacher said.

From that moment on, I threw myself into working harder to improve my dancing. In the last chapter, I mentioned that "working hard" can be a reactive ego strategy. Well, in this case, it absolutely was. Don't get me wrong—hard work is essential for success in almost any endeavor. The real question is: *What's the motivating energy behind the hard work?*

Was I working hard because I loved dancing and it brought me joy? Or was I working hard to disprove my story that I wasn't good enough? Depending on the day, my motivation fluctuated. *And if I wasn't good enough at dancing, what else could that mean about me? Was I not a good enough student? Not a good enough daughter? Did it mean I wasn't a good person—maybe even unlovable?*

Fast-forward through the years. I kept working hard—*so hard*. I danced five days a week throughout high school and into college. In 1998, as a college freshman, I even started teaching dance to faculty members' kids on campus. By my senior year, my dance professor gave me words of encouragement that would have been validating if I had been listening as my higher self. She told me, "Brittany, you can always teach dance, but you won't always be able to perform. You have a gift, and you need to share it."

To anyone else, those words might have sounded like, *You are good enough!* Or even, *You are more than enough!* But Brandi had already etched "not good enough" into my mind like a permanent tattoo. So when people told me the opposite of what I thought was true, I couldn't hear them. Because my college dance professor encouraged me—not because I believed in myself—I moved to Chicago to take a shot at dancing professionally.

It was during my time in Chicago that I experienced what I'd call a sliding door moment.

The "Sliding Door" Moment

After graduating from college in 2002, I moved out of the dorms and into an apartment just north of Chicago, in Evanston, Illinois. My big move was driven by desire to train at the renowned Gus Giordano Jazz Dance Chicago (GGJD) School. It was founded by the legendary Gus Giordano in the 1960s and was famous for its strong jazz dance training. That summer, I signed up for unlimited classes, determined to immerse myself in the dance world. With Brandi's relentless push to work harder, I kept at it day in and day out. By the end of the summer, I auditioned for both the GGJD scholarship program and a professional dance position with Royal Caribbean Cruise Lines. I went to the cruise line audition so I could have my first practice auditioning for a job in the dance world.

To my complete surprise, not only did I get offered the scholarship to GGJD, but I was also offered the job with Royal Caribbean. Oh, how I love a happy ending!

Except... It wasn't the end of the story because Brandi had to have her say in the matter.

Brandi's belief that I wasn't good enough was going to keep nagging at me no matter how many milestones I reached. Here I was in this pivotal moment. I was twenty-two, and I had two opportunities laid out before me. One was to train at a professional dance studio, with the hope of eventually being good enough to get paid for performing. The other was to travel the world, dancing on one of the world's most reputable cruise lines at the time, and get paid handsomely to do what I had worked so hard to do.

You'd think that being offered the dream job on the cruise ship meant Brandi would relax, maybe even let me believe that I was good enough. But no—Brandi wouldn't let me off the hook. Even with people literally telling me to my face, "We would like to hire you. Here's a year-long contract," a.k.a. "We think you are good enough," Brandi's voice still whispered: *You're not ready. You need more training.*

The story Brandi had been feeding me since I was twelve was so powerful that I couldn't hear the truth, even when it was offered to me on a silver platter. So instead of embracing the chance to travel the world and perform, I convinced myself I needed to train more to become good enough—one day.

So, I turned down the Royal Caribbean Cruise Line gig and accepted the scholarship instead.

I know, you're probably shaking your head in disbelief. But don't blame me—blame Brandi. She still doesn't know that I can dance.

So, you think you can dance?!

Within a year, I was rehearsing full-time with the Gus Giordano Jazz Dance Chicago Second Company. I started picking up one-off performances with other dance companies and booking industrial dance gigs.

The industrial work was strange but really fun. One gig had me in a hooded, footed, gloved, silver, shiny Lycra unitard, improvising down a runway with various high-end sink faucets. My job? To "bring the faucets to life." It sounds ridiculous, but it actually took years of training to be able to show up, improvise without rehearsal, work for four hours, and walk away with $800.

Another time, I performed for Thermador, a luxury kitchen appliance brand, at a Kitchen and Bath convention in Chicago. I also danced at an At Home America convention with a crew that included three dancers from the Joffrey Ballet and two from Hubbard Street Dance Chicago. They were some of the most talented dancers around town at the time, and together we pulled off the gig with just one day of rehearsal. The pay for these gigs was ten times more than what we'd make for concert work. Concerts and artistic performances were what I dreamt of as a kid, despite the fact they took months of preparation and typically paid pennies on the dollar compared to the industrial shows. And yet, despite these accomplishments, the nagging story that I wasn't good enough still clung to me. In the back of my mind, I thought I was hired because I was a hard worker—not that I was a talented dancer.

In 2005, I moved to Utah with Derek, where I balanced performing with teaching dance at a college preparatory boarding school. It was there that the real emotional moment of my limiting belief came to a head.

It was 2008, I was twenty-eight, and I auditioned for the reality TV show, *So You Think You Can Dance*. The show was known for discovering incredibly talented dancers and giving them a chance to perform on national television. Getting a "ticket to Vegas" meant you were advancing to the next round, where the competition would be fierce, and the judges would select the best of the best.

I still get emotional when I think about that moment in Salt Lake City. Nigel Lythgoe and Mia Michaels, the judges, didn't know anything about how hard of a worker I was. All they saw was me dancing for two minutes to a beautiful Missy Higgins song and knew that I was a good dancer. There were 2,000 dancers at the audition, and they handed out just twenty-five tickets to Vegas that day—and I was one of them.

It took another five years for me to realize that Brandi's idea that "I'm not good enough" wasn't just a story. *It was a bald-faced lie.*

Eleven years after that, it finally clicked that it was Brandi who fed me that lie all along.

Despite all this, I had a wonderful career as a professional dancer that lasted over fifteen years! I danced my last performance at age thirty-seven when I was eight weeks pregnant with my son, Isaac. His arrival would pull all the skeletons out of the closet and show me other lies Brandi had been telling me my whole life.

What's with all the lies?

In the very brief history lesson in Chapter 1, I introduced ahamkara, the yogic concept of separateness, as described in the Yoga Sutras.

Ahamkara represents the imaginary boundary that defines "me" as distinct from "you"—essentially, the ego self. But it doesn't stop there. Connected to ahamkara is asmita, the tendency to unconsciously choose identities within the boundary to make us feel unique.

Asmita is the mind's way of attaching our sense of identity to external labels, like "I'm a mom" or "I'm smart"—or worse, "I'm stupid." These identity labels create separation and can be either positive or negative, depending on how we choose to define ourselves. As you read in the previous story, Brandi reinforced the identity, "I'm not good enough," for most of my life, and that belief ran deep, shaping how I moved through the world.

Just like a worn path in the grass reveals the footsteps of those who've traveled it many times, these identity beliefs, whether positive or negative, carve deep grooves into our subconscious. In yoga, we call these grooves samskaras. They're the habits and mental patterns that, over time, form our default responses. For me, the samskara of "not being good enough" was like an old, familiar rut. If we keep focusing on the negative, those beliefs become limitations, and we start to feel stuck and unable to evolve.

This concept of limiting beliefs isn't exclusive to yoga—it spans across psychology, personal development, and spirituality. I can see how Brandi's stories about my worth tie into broader teachings, including Cognitive Behavioral Therapy (CBT). My therapist used CBT to invite me to challenge Brandi's narrative by using evidence-based thinking, replacing those old, limiting thoughts with more balanced, accurate beliefs. In CBT, these limiting beliefs are called cognitive distortions—irrational thoughts that warp how we see ourselves and the world. CBT invited me to challenge Brandi's narrative by using evidence-based thinking, replacing those old, limiting thoughts with more balanced, accurate beliefs.

I also find parallels between Brandi's stories and concepts from Neurolinguistic Programming (NLP). In NLP, limiting beliefs are reframed by shifting the language we use to describe ourselves and our experiences. Realizing that by changing how I speak to myself—choosing empowering words over self-deprecating ones—I can start to break free from Brandi's narrative.

This reframe reminds me of the importance of focusing on my strengths, something that Positive Psychology emphasizes. The shift from what's wrong to what's right mirrors what I had to do with Brandi. Positive Psychology, led by scholars like Martin Seligman, focuses on cultivating positive emotions and strengths, which counteract the effects of limiting beliefs. Instead of focusing on what I lack, I can focus on what I can celebrate about myself, however small.

Beyond psychology, spirituality also plays a key role in helping me confront Brandi's stories. Teachers like Eckhart Tolle and Louise Hay advocate for mindfulness and affirmations—two practices that have been lifelines for me even before I consciously knew about my limiting beliefs. Tolle teaches that when we stay present, we avoid getting trapped in the mind's stories.

When I bring mindfulness to Brandi's fearful whispers, I'm able to see them as just that—stories, not facts. Meanwhile, Louise Hay's affirmations help me overwrite the old script. Replacing "I'm not good enough" with affirmations like "I'm worthy," shifts my internal dialogue.

Influential voices like Tony Robbins, Brené Brown, and Gabrielle Bernstein also offer insights that help to dismantle limiting beliefs. Tony Robbins focuses on changing our mindset and emotional state. He advocates for rewiring our brain's associations, transforming fear into action. That's exactly what I have to do—move from Brandi's fear-driven mindset to a more empowered, action-oriented one.

Brené Brown's work on vulnerability hits home for me. She teaches that embracing our imperfections and leaning into discomfort allows us to break down shame and self-doubt. I have to get real with myself—acknowledging the shame that Brandi's stories create, while also embracing the courage it takes to choose a new path.

Gabrielle Bernstein's teachings also influence my journey, particularly her spiritual approach of transforming fear into faith. By questioning Brandi's fearful thoughts and surrendering them to a greater purpose, I can shift from a mindset of scarcity to one of abundance.

Here are some common limiting beliefs/lies our egos unconsciously feel or tell us:

"I'm not good enough" is a popular one.
"I'm alone."
"I'm unlovable."
"I'm not worthy," or even more brutal, "I'm worthless," hits a really tender nerve.
"I'm bad."
"I'm weak."
"I'm stupid."
The list could go on and on.

I first learned about my limiting beliefs at the yoga teacher training I attended with Baron Baptiste in 2013. Baron introduced us to a process called Defying the Lie, which challenged the self-imposed limitations and beliefs that held us back from realizing our full potential. It was there that I uncovered the deep-rooted belief of not being good enough that started when I was twelve.

Once I discovered this lie, I began to see it around every corner. It wasn't just a feeling; it was a driving force behind everything I did. I found myself constantly trying to prove it wrong.

Needing to prove something can be motivating.

Trying to prove yourself can be a powerful motivator, and for me, it led to a long list of accomplishments. I could see how I had spent my entire life trying to prove that I was good enough:

- I worked hard to be a straight-A student and graduated near the top of my class in high school.
- I collected all the certifications during my time as a summer camp counselor.
- I graduated from college with honors.
- I danced professionally with various companies in Chicago, Utah, and Colorado.
- I co-built, with my own hands, a 1,200-square-foot straw bale house and lived in it.
- I drove a car that ran on waste vegetable oil.
- I created two dance programs: one for a college prep boarding school in Utah and another for an international school in Beijing, China.
- I started a small business that grew from offering free yoga in the park to a team of eighteen, serving thousands of yoga students over the course of seven years.

While I truly wanted to achieve all of those things because I cared and was passionate, I also accomplished them because I was capable. So again, the limiting belief that I wasn't good enough was a lie. But Brandi was there at almost every step, pushing me to prove something and not believe people when they said how proud they were of me, or that they loved what I was teaching. I wonder what it would have been like if Brandi wasn't constantly driving me to work so hard to disprove the lie. Would I have still achieved the same success, but with more ease and joy? What would it have felt like if I wasn't constantly paddling upstream?

All of those accomplishments came at a cost. There was an exhausting undercurrent, a pressure to prove that I was good enough, which often took the joy out of the journey. Without Brandi, I imagine I would have worked with the same dedication, but without that constant sense of urgency, without the feeling that my worth was on the line with every step I took.

To illustrate the pressure I put on myself and how I unconsciously let Brandi take the lead, I'll share another story. It's a perfect example of how striving to disprove the lie—that I wasn't good enough—can lead to success, but also at significant personal costs like health, peace of mind, and joy.

It's exhausting trying to prove the lie wrong.

My heart was racing. It felt like everything around me was closing in. I was six months into my yoga business at age thirty-seven when I had my first panic attack.

I was sitting in the parking lot of a hardware store, talking to my ever-supportive mom, when my chest continued to tighten, and I struggled to catch my breath.

"Do you think maybe you're having a panic attack?" she asked gently.

I quickly dismissed the idea—*me? A panic attack? I owned a yoga studio. I meditated regularly. I was supposed to be grounded and graceful in every moment.* But the truth was undeniable: I had a lot on my plate, and the pressure I was putting on myself was suffocating.

I had just moved from China to Denver. I was living off my savings and had started the yoga business by offering free yoga classes in the park, gradually building a community from scratch. That week, I had signed a one-year lease on a studio space I could barely afford and launched a crowdfunding campaign to cover the rent. The weight of making the business succeed pressed down on me like a vice. I couldn't fail.

The following years were a whirlwind of exhilaration and exhaustion. I built an incredible team, led workshops, yoga teacher trainings, and retreats, and even bought the very building I had rented. Four years into this journey, I gave birth to my son, Isaac, and continued to run the business, with our family living in an apartment tucked in the back of the yoga studio.

My stepmom recently reminded me of a visit when Isaac was just four months old. She had come to help watch him during one of my yoga teacher training weekends. "You were on your lunch break during the twelve-hour training day, pumping milk for Isaac while eating your lunch and meeting with the studio manager," she said, with a look that spoke volumes about the intensity of that time.

Looking back, the toll on my health and well-being was painfully clear. That first summer of COVID, I led 900 hours of online yoga teacher trainings, taught regular weekly scheduled classes on Zoom, and navigated a divorce, all while raising a toddler.

By August of 2021, the business had made it seven years and I was utterly drained. I reached a crossroads: either rebuild the business after losing three-quarters of the memberships to lockdowns and masks in the pandemic, or sell the property and finally rest. The community, ever supportive, urged me to keep going. They wanted me to keep being the person who showed up for them. But deep down, I knew I was running on fumes. A new lie, courtesy of Brandi, whispered in my ear: *If I close, I will be failing them.*

But I had to face the truth: I was now a single mom—selling the building would allow me to take two years off and focus on my son and my health. I succeeded in proving I was good enough, but the cost of the charade was too high. I couldn't keep sacrificing for others at the expense of myself and my little family.

Looking back, I can see how operating from the need to prove the lie wrong had driven me to succeed, but it had also cost me my health, peace of mind, and happiness, even in moments of success. I wouldn't change the experience of sharing yoga with so many people through Container Collective Yoga. But if I could do it again, I'd approach it differently. I'd move from the energy of knowing how capable I am— not from the need to prove that I'm capable.

Is your ego self like Brandi—driven by the need to prove the lie wrong? For many, this drive can feel like it's serving them, just as it did me. It can be a motivational force, the wind in your sails pushing you to do more, be better, and get stronger. Get good grades. Win awards. Climb the career ladder. Achieve success in whatever areas you've unconsciously decided will prove your worth—no matter the cost.

Maybe you relate. Or maybe you don't. If not, there's a good chance you're operating from a space of proving the lie right.

Prove the lie "right," and you get a cookie!

But why would anyone want to be right about limiting beliefs like being weak, alone, or unworthy? The answer lies in how the brain works—specifically, dopamine.

Dopamine is often called the "feel-good" chemical in the brain because it creates sensations of pleasure and reward. It's well documented that the brain releases dopamine when our expectations are met, leading to a sense of satisfaction—even when those expectations reinforce limiting beliefs.

Here's the kicker: It's not just about being *factually* right. You don't have to *actually* be right—you just have to *feel* right. When your beliefs or predictions line up with what you think is true, it triggers a dopamine release. This can reinforce behaviors, like seeking out situations or making choices that align with those beliefs, which make you *feel* right.

My teacher, Baron Baptiste, calls this "getting a cookie for being right." It's an intriguing unconscious reward system that can keep us stuck in limiting beliefs because, believe it or not, your brain can get a dopamine hit when you're proven right about a limiting belief, even if the outcome feels negative.

For example, let's say I'm in college and my ego holds the belief that I'm stupid. I might procrastinate, avoid studying, or even self-sabotage in some way like going out and partying instead of studying and resting the night before an exam. Then, when I fail the test, instead of feeling like I just didn't prepare well enough, Brandi pipes up with, *See? I knew I wasn't smart enough.* The failure stings, but in a strange way, it also validates the belief, giving me that "cookie" of being right.

Or, if I have a limiting belief that I'm not lovable, I might find myself in relationships with people who don't treat me well or aren't emotionally available. When those relationships inevitably fall apart, even though it's painful, Brandi might say, *I knew this wouldn't work out*. And there's that little hit of dopamine again—I "get the cookie" of being right, even if it comes at the cost of reinforcing a belief that keeps me stuck.

I remember a time when this cycle played out in my own life. In the early days of building my yoga business, I was constantly stressed about whether it would succeed. Deep down, Brandi whispered that I wasn't good enough to make it work. Whenever something went wrong—a class with low attendance, a dip in the finances—Brandi would jump in with, *See? I knew I couldn't do it*. As disheartening as it was, I'd feel this strange sense of validation because at least I was "right" about my fears.

This need to be "right" about my limiting beliefs didn't just show up in my business; it bled into my relationships, too. If a friend didn't reach out for a while, Brandi would say, *They don't really care about you*. And even when that friend eventually texted or called, instead of feeling relief, I was already stuck in the belief that their absence proved I wasn't important to them.

These are just a few examples of how our unconscious reward system can reinforce the lies we tell ourselves, making it harder to break free from the cycle. But the good news? We can change this pattern by becoming aware of it. The first step is recognizing that the "cookie" isn't worth the cost. Once you see that, you can start shifting from a place of fear and limitation to one of empowerment and possibility.

This next practice is designed to help you uncover the limiting beliefs—or lies—that your ego may be telling you. These beliefs often operate below the surface, subtly shaping how you see yourself and interact with the world. By bringing them to light, you can begin to understand where they come from, how they've influenced your behavior, and most importantly, how you can start shifting them. This exercise is adapted from what I learned at my first yoga teacher training with Baron Baptiste, and he includes a version of it in his book, *Being of Power*.

Practice #6: Identify Your Limiting Beliefs, or Lies

As I've said before, I truly believe in the power of yoga, which includes mindful movement, intentional breathing, meditation, and self-inquiry. These practices have been transformative for me, but I also want to emphasize that they don't replace the incredible support that comes from working with a licensed therapist when you're diving into deeper emotional work. This exercise is a powerful way to begin uncovering and challenging the beliefs that might be holding you back.

In your journal, journaling app, or <u>free workbook</u>:

Part 1: Get present

1. **Check in physically:** Take a deep breath in and out. Notice how you feel physically, and write down your observations.

    If you need to, you can add the phrase, "It makes sense that you feel that way."

2. **Check in mentally/emotionally:** Take another deep breath in and out. Write down how you're feeling mentally and emotionally.

    Again, if it resonates, add, "It makes sense that you feel that way."

3. **Speak to your ego self:** Fill in the blank with your ego's name, and say the following:

    "_____, we're about to do an exercise that is meant to be supportive. You might get triggered and want to react, but I'm here for us. You're not being punished, and you don't have to go anywhere. I've got us. We're just going to become aware of some habits that we can shift so we feel better in our day-to-day lives."

If that statement doesn't feel right, feel free to adjust it to something that feels supportive for you.

Part 2: Identify the limiting beliefs

Think of a few moments recently where you found yourself reacting to a situation or person, instead of acting with intention.

Set a timer for sixty seconds, and use that time to list the limiting beliefs or words that come to mind when you think about the situation(s).

Example list:

- *I'm not good enough.*
- *I'm stupid.*
- *I'm not important.*
- *I'm alone.*
- *I don't matter.*
- *I'm not worthy, or I'm worthless.*
- *I'm not lovable.*
- *I'm bad.*

Part 3: Focus on one limiting belief

Pick one belief from your list that stings the most when you think about it. Circle it or highlight it so it stands out.

Did you choose one?

Time travel list:

1. **Last one to twelve months:** Think about a time in the last year when this belief showed up. Can you recall a specific incident? Give it a title and have it be the first bullet point on your list.

2. **Two to five years ago:** Travel back in your mind two to five years. When did this belief show up in your life during that time? Add another bullet point with a title for the situation(s).

3. **Ten-plus years ago:** Go back ten or more years. When do you remember feeling this way? Write down another bullet point for that memory.

4. **Childhood:** Now travel to your childhood. Can you pinpoint the first time you remember feeling this way? How old were you? Write in as much or as little detail as you'd like about this experience.

Part 4: Fact vs. Meaning

In that childhood memory, can you separate the facts from the story your younger self made up?

Example:

- **Fact:** "My dance teacher said, 'It's sweet how much she loves to dance. Too bad she'll never go anywhere with it.'"
- **What I made it mean:** "I'm not good enough."

Take a moment to reflect: **Can you see how your younger self turned ego self has been holding on to this story, whispering it in your ear all your life?**

Part 5: Proving it Right or Wrong

Create two columns in your journal (or if you're using a digital app, just create two headings):

Column One: Ways my ego tried to prove the limiting belief, or lie, "right."

Column Two: Ways my ego tried to prove the limiting belief, or lie, "wrong."

Example:

Ways Brandi tried to prove the limiting belief, or lie, "I'm not good enough," wrong:

- Worked hard to get straight A's.
- Graduated with honors.
- Worked hard at dancing.
- Started a business.

Ways Brandi tried to prove the limiting belief, or lie, "I'm not good enough," right:

- Stayed in a relationship where I wasn't authentic for sixteen years.

We will reframe the lies—the limiting beliefs—later in the chapter.

In the meantime, take a moment to reflect on the letter you wrote to your ego self in Chapter 2. Remember, while your ego has cost you some things, it has also given you certain strengths. Recognizing both can help you move forward with compassion.

Notice how these beliefs show up in your day-to-day life.

As you continue to witness, you may discover new limiting beliefs that surface. When that happens, you can revisit this process to allow your higher self to take the lead with compassion.

Which of the following best describes your ego's general way of being in the world?

1. Your ego has helped you achieve many great things over the years. However, operating in the energy of "reaction to a limiting belief" hasn't been the most empowering way to move through life. It may have cost you peace, joy, health, or other important aspects of well-being.

2. Your ego has kept you from engaging fully in life. The limiting beliefs you've been reacting to have kept you stuck and held you back from taking action in many areas of your life.

Regardless of which resonates with you—whether your ego has driven you to overachieve or held you back—keep this in mind. This next section will look at some clues that tell you when your ego is trying to help you by taking command, even though it's not actually very helpful.

Ego Statements

I was at my third week-long yoga teacher training when Baron put us in toes pose. If you've never tried it, toes pose sounds innocent enough—it's just a kneeling position, with your toes curled under to stretch the bottoms of both feet. For a few seconds, maybe even a minute, it's fine. You might even enjoy the stretch. But then Baron told us to stay in it for ten minutes— that's when the nice stretch stopped. Toes pose quickly earned its nickname: screaming toes pose.

At first, it was just a mild discomfort, but then the sensation started to build, like a fire spreading across the bottoms of my feet. Every minute felt like an eternity. Baron invited us to pay attention to the thoughts, phrases, and statements that popped into our minds as the intensity grew. Every time thoughts came up, we were asked to write them down in our journals and then return to the pose. Simple, right?

Well, not exactly. The longer I stayed in the pose, the louder Brandi became. My journal entries from those ten minutes went from mild irritation to pure rebellion:

"This is stupid."
"You don't understand."
"This sucks."
"I don't want to do this anymore."

It wasn't just me. As I glanced around the room, I could see the same struggle written across pretty much everyone else's faces. Later, some of my fellow participants shared their thoughts, and they were just as colorful:

"You're stupid."
"Don't tell me what to do."

"You're wrong."
"Screw you!"
"Leave me alone."

These statements were clues—signs that our ego selves were getting triggered. Brandi wasn't happy, and she wanted out. The discomfort of the pose wasn't just physical; it brought up all the feelings she'd been trying to avoid. Phrases like, "This sucks," or "I don't want to do this," were her ways of trying to take control, so she didn't have to feel "not good enough" or like she "didn't matter."

It was the ego's defense mechanism kicking in, commanding the situation to change so I wouldn't feel so vulnerable.

Brandi even began looking around the room to make sure she wasn't the only one having a hard time.

Sometimes, these ego statements spill out of our mouths, while other times, they're running through our heads, making chatter that's louder than anything else, especially the steady voice of the higher self.

Still during other instances, nothing may be thought or felt at all.

There was one fellow trainee who didn't write a single thing down while she was in toes pose. She sat there, toes curled under, completely still, her face calm and expressionless. I couldn't tell if the pose simply didn't bother her, if her ego was so determined to stay hidden that it refused to reveal anything, or if she had slipped into a freeze state.

It made me wonder: What was going on beneath her composed exterior? Was her ego so well guarded that it managed to suppress every rebellious thought, every flicker of discomfort? Or had she simply shut down, her mind and body frozen in response to the intensity?

Sometimes, when the pressure becomes too much, we don't fight or flee—we freeze. The ego triggers the nervous system into serious survival mode, and everything goes quiet, locking up to protect us from whatever feels overwhelming.

I'm also open to the possibility that maybe her higher self had managed to step in, keeping her centered and calm in the storm of the pose. Wouldn't that be amazing to be that wise in the eye of a storm? But to Brandi, that felt like the least likely scenario. She couldn't help but wonder (for me) what that woman's experience was like in those ten minutes of screaming toes pose.

The ego can be tricky. Sometimes it hides in plain sight, avoiding discovery by going quiet instead of lashing out.

While I never did hear that woman's truth about the experience, Brandi's observations effectively reminded me that not everyone's ego reacts the same way in discomfort. Some egos scream and rebel, like Brandi sometimes does, while others slip into silence, waiting for the storm to pass. Either way, the clues are there if we're paying attention.

If you're curious about what your ego self might say in moments of discomfort, you're welcome to try "screaming toes pose" or even a wall-sit for ten minutes. If you find yourself just leaving the pose and not staying the entire time, try having someone join you in the process as an accountability buddy. It's a powerful way to see what comes up. But don't worry, if that sounds like too much, I have an exercise coming up after the next story that will help you hear your ego statements without the intense toe or thigh fire!

Brandi Wants to be Understood

I remember one of the first times I distinctly heard Brandi say, *But you don't understand,* inside my head. I had just returned home after that week of training with the toes pose exercise. A customer, Linda, emailed me, asking for a refund on her membership. She was upset because I had changed the time of a class on the weekly schedule.

When I was running the yoga studio, memberships were the key to predictable monthly revenue. Scheduling classes was like a delicate balancing act—figuring out which times would serve the most people. I had decided to shift a class start time by thirty minutes, from 4:00 p.m. to 4:30 p.m., thinking it would accommodate more community members. But Linda, a regular attendee, was not okay with the change. She emailed immediately after the announcement to cancel her membership, saying the new time didn't work for her.

As soon as I read her email, the words echoed in my mind almost immediately: *But you don't understand. I'm trying to run a business here, and I need to...*

Brandi was triggered and knew how to take control and be in command of the situation. It doesn't even matter what came after that—everything Brandi was about to say was driven by the need to prove something. If I had let Brandi take over, she would have crafted a response that dismissed Linda's frustration. It would have defended my decision and justified why I changed the class time, while subtly telling Linda, *You don't understand what I'm going through as a small business owner.*

Brandi's response would have come from the place of trying to prove the limiting belief, or lies, "I'm not good enough," or "I don't matter," wrong, depending on the story she was running with that day.

But here's where it gets tricky. Who's to say Linda's ego self wasn't also at play? When she saw that schedule change, maybe her own ego statement kicked in—something like, "I don't matter," or "No one cares about my needs." Maybe her ego, not Linda, was the one who sent that email, reacting to her own belief that she wasn't important. It's possible that her email was an unconscious attempt to regain control over something that made her feel like she didn't matter.

So there we were, two ego selves bumping up against each other, both trying to maintain control of the situation. Brandi, ready to fire off a defensive email, and Linda's ego, feeling wronged by the schedule change. Do you see the potential chain reaction that could have unraveled from this? It's fascinating how something as small as a yoga class time change can snowball into a conflict of wills. And when you zoom out to other scenarios—like someone getting cut off in traffic or their preferred candidate losing an election—the chain reactions of ego-driven responses start to look even more wild and chaotic.

But here's the thing: In that moment I read Linda's email, I had a clue. I heard Brandi's statement: *But you don't understand.* And that recognition was my saving grace. I paused. I took a deep breath and acknowledged what was really happening—Brandi was trying to take control. She was reacting to the lie that she wasn't good enough, and she wanted to defend herself. But I didn't have to let her.

Instead, I consciously chose to respond as Brittany, not Brandi. I replied to Linda with kindness and understanding. I validated her frustration about the schedule change and explained the reason behind it, but I also let her know that I valued her as a member of our community. I offered a solution that would allow her to keep her membership, maybe by trying a different class time or a virtual option. And if those options didn't work, I was okay to refund the charge.

At that moment, my higher self was in charge. I didn't need to prove anything. I didn't need to defend or justify myself. I simply wanted to find a way to keep the connection with Linda intact, while honoring the business decision I had made.

This awareness of ego statements as reactive thoughts or phrases that pop up in challenging situations can be incredibly valuable. Recognizing them in real time allows us to pause, breathe, and choose a response aligned with our higher self, rather than our triggered ego self.

To help you identify your own ego statements, I invite you to try out this next practice.

Practice #7: Identify Your Ego Statements

This practice is adapted from an exercise in *The Book of Forgiving* by Desmond Tutu.

Find a relatively, or completely, smooth rock that will comfortably fit in the palm of your hand. It shouldn't be so big that you can't use your hand to pick something light up, but also not so small that you'll easily lose it.

Identify the limiting belief, or lie, you worked with in the last practice and have the rock represent that limiting belief, or lie.

Now, to the "fun" part, which will lead you to identify your ego statements.

1. **Choose a day or time to hold the rock in your nondominant hand for six hours.**
   - First notice what you thought when you read the last sentence. It may be your first clue to one of your ego statements.
   - If you really want to get the most out of this exercise, don't set the rock down for any reason for the entire six hours.

- Write down in your journal, or your notes app, the "charged" phrase(s) that come up for you over the six hours. Write it down, even if it happens multiple times. Those statements will be important to recognize.

Examples: "This is stupid." "I don't need this."

2. **After you've held the rock in your nondominant hand for six hours, journal with the following prompts:**
   - When did you notice the limiting belief or ego statements the most?
   - In what ways did the limiting belief or ego statements limit you throughout the six hours?
   - Was the limiting belief or were the ego statements ever useful?
   - How does this six-hour exercise parallel the impact of your limiting beliefs on your life as a whole?
   - Can you see the possibility of more ego statements presenting themselves moving forward?

What to do with Your Discoveries

Now that you've identified some of your ego statements, it's important to understand how they influence your behavior and how you can begin to shift them.

→ **Awareness:** Acknowledge your ego statements when they arise in your daily life. Simply being aware of them is the first step toward change. Notice when they pop up and how they make you feel.

→ **Pause and Reflect:** When you catch yourself in a moment where an ego statement surfaces, pause. Take a deep breath, and instead of reacting immediately, take a walk or journal to reflect on whether this statement is serving you or reinforcing the limiting belief, or lie. Is it helpful to say to yourself, "It makes sense that you feel..."?

→ **Practice Compassion:** Remember that these ego statements are your ego's way of trying to protect you, even if they're not always helpful. Offer yourself compassion and understanding, recognizing that these patterns developed for a reason, but you now have the tools to change them.

→ **Regular Reflection:** Notice if new ego statements show up or if old ones start to lose their power. Notice if there are certain times or situations that typically trigger these thoughts. (We will dive deeper into this awareness later in the book.)

You can take the insights gained from this practice and turn them into meaningful change in your life. Over time, as you become more aware of your ego statements and learn to reframe them, you'll find yourself responding to challenges with greater calm and clarity, allowing your higher self to take the lead.

Remember that your ego statements are important; because they're clues for you to see when your ego might be trying to whisper in your ear, drive the car, or take the lead in your life.

When you catch it, you can do the next practice to empower your higher self to stop the chain reaction.

Empowered Statements = Another Way of Operating

By now you've probably started noticing the patterns of what your ego tends to say and feel. If you've done all of the practices up to this point, you likely understand why your ego acts the way it does—based on your past experiences. You're likely seeing how often you have let your ego be in charge.

But here's the million-dollar question: How do you, as your higher self, regain the driver's seat of the car once you see it happening?

One method that's been incredibly helpful for me is creating empowered statements. These come from a place of deep intention, and they're often the exact opposite of the limiting beliefs or lies that your ego has been reacting to.

Here's an example of what happens weekly between me and Brandi. My husband will come home from work, set his computer bag down, and immediately the dog and kids rush to him with excitement. I've been home with the crew for hours, keeping everyone fed and entertained while attempting to keep some semblance of order in the house. By this point, I'm usually tired and I'd love to be greeted with a hug or a kiss. Most days, he does. But some days, it doesn't happen right away. When it doesn't, Brandi is quick to pull out one of her statements: *What about me? Everyone else gets pets and smiles. What am I, chopped liver?*

"What about me?" is one of my ego statements when Brandi feels like she doesn't matter. I've learned to be aware of it. Under the surface, I can feel the lie: *I don't matter.*

If left unchecked, anything that comes after "What about me?" will likely lead to a spiral of resentment and possibly a fight. However, recognizing that statement is my clue that Brandi is running the show, so I am able to step in, knowing that *I do matter.*

One way I reclaim the narrative is to take a deep breath, wiggle my toes to physically arrive in the present moment, and say to myself an empowered statement like, "I give up the lie that I don't matter, and I create myself as worthy." With the understanding that I do matter, I can act differently. Instead of stewing over Brandi's feeling of being overlooked, I can authentically reach out to Adam for a hug or kiss. Or I can even ask, "Can I have a hug?" Brandi may feel vulnerable asking, but my higher self knows I'm worth it. And if he's not able to do it right away, I know his affection is just around the corner.

This is also a yogic concept, called sankalpa, that is not limited to use on the yoga mat at a yoga studio; it can be used in everyday life.

Sankalpa

A great way to think of empowered statements is as a modernized variation of the yogic practice of sankalpa. For those unfamiliar, sankalpa is a Sanskrit word that translates to "intention" or "resolve." It's a positive declaration or affirmation aligned with your higher purpose and deepest desires. When yoga teachers ask you to set an intention at the beginning of class, they're inviting you to create your own sankalpa for your practice. A sankalpa is also a tool you can use at any moment in your life.

Here are the key aspects of sankalpa and how they relate to both your ego self and higher self:

- **Purposeful Intention:** Unlike the ego self, which often operates from fear, doubt, or a need to prove something, sankalpa comes from a deeper place—a place of true intention. It reflects your higher self's aspirations and goals, not the ego's reactive desires. While your ego self might want to prove you're worthy by achieving external success, your higher self sets an intention that aligns with your inner purpose and authentic desires.

- **Present Tense:** The ego is frequently caught up in the past— regretting mistakes and failures. Some egos spend time in the future, worrying about what might happen. A sankalpa brings you into the present moment. It's stated as if it's already happening, because your higher self operates in the now. Instead of the ego-driven, "I will be healthy one day," your higher self declares, "I am healthy," fully embracing what is true of your potential in the present moment.

- **Positive Affirmation:** While the ego self often focuses on what's wrong, what's missing, or what needs to be fixed, a sankalpa is a positive affirmation that shifts your attention to what you want to bring into your life. The higher self doesn't operate from lack or negativity; it sees abundance and possibility. Instead of the ego's mindset of "I need to eliminate this problem," your higher self says, "I invite growth, healing, and joy into my life."

- **Alignment with Higher Self:** A sankalpa naturally aligns with your higher self, channeling your energy toward your deeper sense of purpose. It's a commitment to rise above the ego's short-term desires or fears and tap into what truly matters. While the ego may be focused on external validation or moving away from what it doesn't want, the higher self is committed to living with purpose and intention, moving you toward what you want.

- **Regular Practice:** The ego can be easily distracted or disheartened when things don't go perfectly right away. But your higher self understands that transformation comes with consistency. Incorporating your sankalpa into daily practices—whether through yoga on the mat (asana), on a cushion (meditation), or throughout your day (mindfulness), you are reinforcing your intention and helping bring it to life. The higher self knows that progress is achieved through regular, intentional practice, creating lasting change and deep fulfillment.

With regular practice, you can rewire your brain, creating new neurological pathways— what yogis call *positive samskaras*— replacing those old negative ruts with happy grooves of empowerment.

By identifying and acknowledging your limiting beliefs, you're already halfway there. You've become conscious of how your ego tries to help you and take control of a situation where the limiting belief is triggered by using ego statements.

This next practice is all about taking what you've learned so far and using it to create a new, more powerful way of operating through empowered statements. These intentional affirmations will counteract the lies your ego has been telling you, helping you to create a new narrative for yourself—one where your higher self is in charge.

Practice #8: Create Your Empowered Statements

Recall a moment in the past few days when you felt uneasy or dissatisfied. Maybe your ego self was activated, and you were unconsciously reacting rather than taking action.

1. **Write out a short description of the scenario.**
2. **Speaking to your ego self, fill in the blanks:** I see and acknowledge that you felt _____ (Insert the limiting belief).

Examples:

   - I acknowledge that you felt like you didn't matter.
   - I see that you felt like a failure.
   - I acknowledge that you felt stupid.
   - I see that you felt unlovable and worthless.

3. **That is a story, a lie, that you made up when I was _____ years old.**

Example:

   - That is a story you made up when I was six years old.

4. **Complete the following sentence:**

   - I choose to create myself as _____(Insert how you want to feel or be; perhaps it's the literal opposite of the limiting belief, or something else.).

Examples:

- Right now, I create myself as more than enough.
- Right now, I create myself as capable and strong.
- Right now, I create myself as worthy.

After you've created your empowered statement, take a moment to let it sink in.

How does it feel to choose this new way of being? You may want to write it down somewhere visible, repeat it to yourself daily, or use it as an affirmation you repeat during meditation.

One way to reframe the limiting belief is to write it out with your empowered statement four times. This exercise falls within the Neurolinguistic Programming (NLP) therapy world; I've also adapted some pieces from motivational speaker, Lisa Nichols's, exercise called Expose the Lies.

Example:
I'm not good enough. I'm capable and strong.
I'm not good enough. I'm capable and strong.
I'm not good enough. I'm capable and strong.
I'm not good enough. I'm capable and strong.

Set timers in your phone to read the list four times a day, for two days.

Then on the third day, erase or cross out the limiting belief and read just the empowered statement four times in a row four times that day.

Example:
I'm capable and strong.
I'm capable and strong.
I'm capable and strong.
I'm capable and strong.

It's fascinating to watch what begins to happen in the brain when you do this final part of the process.

The more you practice affirming your new belief, the more it will become integrated into your life. Over time, you'll notice a shift in how you respond to situations that once triggered your ego. By consistently using your empowered statement, you're letting your higher self take the lead and guide your life in a direction that feels authentic and aligned with your true self.

I love how author and teacher Danielle Laporte says we can't just slap affirmations like, "I'm strong," or "I'm beautiful," onto ourselves in toxically positive ways because our nervous system will reject them.

> It's like our ego self has a built-in bullshit meter. When we try to force affirmations that don't align with the stories our ego believes about us, that meter goes off.

For example, saying, "I'm gorgeous!" when Brandi has been running with the belief "I'm ugly" sets off alarm bells in the form of discomfort, doubt, or straight-up rejection of the affirmation.

This happens because the nervous system is tied to the ego's deeply held stories, and it knows when something doesn't match up. The ego has spent years, maybe decades, crafting its narrative about who you are, so when you try to throw an affirmation on top of those limiting beliefs, it's like putting sprinkles on poop and calling it delicious. The ego reacts, and the bullshit meter activates.

Instead of letting the ego take control when this happens, use the tools you've learned so far to recognize how you're actually feeling. When you sense that resistance or discomfort from the ego, pause. Acknowledge what's being activated. Take some intentional breaths, and ask yourself: *How am I feeling physically right now? How am I feeling mentally and emotionally? It makes sense that I feel that way. Right now, I give up the lie _____, and I create myself as _____.*

From this new place of awareness, rather than being stuck in reactive mode with your ego unconsciously spewing statements, your higher self can guide the action. You will think more clearly as you take conscious action.

If you're anything like Brandi, you might be tempted to just read through the practices and not actually do them. Or maybe you've tried something similar in the past and skip to the next section without fully diving in.

But trust me, these practices are here for a reason, and I highly recommend that you give them a shot—*today* or as soon as you can. Even if it feels uncomfortable or unnecessary, try them out in this format. You never know what new insights or breakthroughs might come from putting them into practice.

You may want to do them with a trusted friend, a therapist, or even a partner for added support and accountability. If that sounds like a good option for you, go for it! And if you want to work with me, or someone on my team directly, I'd love to support you on this journey—don't hesitate to reach out.

However you choose to approach these practices, the important thing is to *just do them.* They're designed to help you dig deeper, and they'll set the foundation for getting even more out of the tools I share in the next chapter. So take the leap—you've got this!

Action Steps for Chapter 3

Remember to be kind to yourself as you work through challenging your limiting beliefs. If it's helpful, share your limiting beliefs and new empowered statements with a trusted friend, mentor, or therapist. Getting external feedback can provide additional insights and encouragement.

- Practice #6: Identify Your Limiting Beliefs, or Lies
- Practice #7: Identify Your Ego Statements
- Practice #8: Create Your Empowered Statements

You'll be able to identify and challenge limiting beliefs, replace them with empowering statements, and cultivate a positive and growth-oriented mindset in no time.

In Summary

Reflecting on these practices and insights has allowed me to uncover the unconscious lies I've believed about myself and begin rewriting those stories. By acknowledging the ego statements and creating empowered statements, I've learned to let my higher self take the lead more often. This shift has brought more peace, clarity, and authenticity into my life.

Moving Forward

It's important to continue recognizing the role our ego self plays in different situations. In the next chapter, we'll dive into The Drama Triangle and explore how the ego positions us as the victim, persecutor, or rescuer. We'll also discover The Empowerment Dynamic®, which offers us a way to shift into the roles of creator, challenger, and coach—empowering not only ourselves but those around us, too.

Let's keep moving forward on this journey toward deeper self-awareness and more purposeful action.

CHAPTER 4

The Drama of Life

Before diving into the complexities of The Drama Triangle and The Empowerment Dynamic®, take a moment to reflect on your journey so far. Hopefully, you've been engaging with the practices, naming your ego, recognizing the lies it tells, and identifying the ego statements that pop up when it tries to take control. As you've uncovered the limiting beliefs that shape your behaviors and interactions, you now flip the narrative with your empowered statements. These insights are the foundation for understanding how drama and empowerment play out in your life.

In this chapter, we'll explore two of my favorite tools: The Drama Triangle and The Empowerment Dynamic. These frameworks will provide you with practical ways to navigate challenging situations with more clarity and less drama—leading you toward feeling more empowered and peaceful.

I'll start with a story to illustrate how I used this chapter's tools to get out of the drama and into empowerment.

Expectation Breeds Drama

Showing up with expectations is a surefire recipe for disappointment with a dash of drama. Have you ever found yourself attached to an outcome? Like when you expect everything to be "just so," and when it's not, your reaction sets off a chain reaction.

I often find myself on the receiving end of those expectations, especially when leading yoga teacher trainings. I run twenty-five-hour training weekends, and sometimes I open up a sixty-minute asana class to the public during the training weekend, so the studio can continue serving the larger community while we use the space the rest of the time.

One such training weekend, a woman (not in yoga teacher training) named Sharon walked in for class, visibly upset that the room wasn't heated to her usual 103 degrees.

In the rush of transitioning from the teacher training meditation session to the public community hot yoga class, I forgot to turn the heat up. I was already feeling rushed in the quick transition, but what happened next gave me a lesson in ego work I didn't expect.

Sharon huffed back into the lobby from the studio, visibly irritated, and asked my assistant, Janie, if the heat was going to be turned up, or else she'd come to a later class.

Janie, caught off guard by Sharon's intensity and furrowed brow, responded with a warm smile. "Absolutely! You're in the right place, and you're going to sweat!"

At this point in the yoga teacher training, all the trainees knew about Brandi, and most had named their egos, too.

A few of the trainees were on break in the lobby, and exchanged knowing glances in reaction to Sharon's demanding energy. Their ego selves clearly had opinions about this intense person who seemed obsessed with the yoga room's temperature.

Sharon came back into the studio and stationed herself near the door, making sure it was tightly closed behind every student. I didn't notice at first, but she had shut the door in a few people's faces, so determined to keep every degree of heat trapped inside.

Soon enough, Sharon approached me directly. With a forceful tone, she asked, "Are you the teacher?"

Her energy was sharp, and while it threw me off a little, I smiled and replied, "Yes, hi! I'm Brittany!"

She persisted: "Is this going to be a hot yoga class? If not, I'll just come back to the later class."

I felt Brandi's feathers ruffle, but I calmly reassured Sharon, "The heat is set to ninety-two, and the humidity is at 65 percent."

Brandi couldn't resist adding, "I'll get your body moving so you can create a sweat on your own as well!"

Brandi wasn't done. I turned to one of the teacher trainees sitting on a yoga mat nearby and asked, "You get sweaty in this class, don't you?"

The trainee, eager to rescue me, chimed in, "Yes! Totally! I get really sweaty!"

From across the room, another trainee's ego self was already getting defensive, irritated by Sharon's energy and her focus on the temperature. I could feel the subtle undercurrent of tension building.

The heat was still creeping up when class began, but it was still twenty degrees cooler than Sharon's desired 103. Brandi and I took turns taking the lead during the opening of the class, which had the theme of being "playful." Brandi, of course, started second-guessing that theme, especially since Sharon didn't seem to have the energy to embrace playfulness. I had to remind Brandi that there were twenty other students in the room who were there to receive the lesson, not just Sharon.

Brandi, however, kept wanting to check in with Sharon, to make sure she was enjoying herself, or at least starting to sweat. I kept redirecting Brandi's attention back to the class as a whole, grounding myself in the intention to serve everyone present.

Then, about twenty minutes in, Brandi, still clinging to the idea of pleasing Sharon, decided to casually ask the whole class, "Is everyone starting to get hot yet?" But it wasn't everyone Brandi was asking—it was Sharon.

The teacher trainees, supportive as ever, proudly declared, "YES!" But Sharon? She waited a beat, and then, loud and clear, she answered, "NO!"

At that point, I giggled to myself, realizing Brandi had taken the lead again. With that awareness, I took a deep breath and got Brandi back under control, allowing Brittany—my higher self—to lead the rest of the class.

At the end, Sharon left the room quickly, without saying a word to anyone. And Brandi, of course, immediately reached for control. She loves to be acknowledged after class, even with a simple "Thank you for class." But I redirected her to focus on the beautiful energy left in the room and the post-yoga glow everyone else had on their faces.

The cherry on top of my lesson in ego work that day came when Janie approached me during our break. "I'm so proud of myself," she said with a grin. "Sharon was halfway out the door, and I called out, 'Have a great day, Sharon!'"

I raised an eyebrow, wondering about her ego (Janet), and asked, "Did you, Janie, wish her a good day, or did Janet?"

Janie paused, laughed, and admitted, "You're totally right. It was Janet being fake nice."

I couldn't help but smile. Sharon had been a challenging presence that day, but it felt like she was there for a reason, helping all of us learn something important about ourselves and how our egos react when expectations aren't met.

Step One is Acknowledging the Current Reality

I can't tell you how grateful I am that Sharon brought her expectations to class that day. Thanks to her, the trainees got to witness firsthand the shifts I sometimes make between Brittany and Brandi. And because they knew their own ego names, it created a safe space for them to call out their own less-than-ideal, unconscious reactions to Sharon's energy.

Looking back, I see how perfectly that class unfolded for all of us to learn and grow. Brandi bumped up against Sharon's strong desire for the room temperature to meet her exact expectations, and Sharon's vocal demands felt like a direct attack on Brandi, who quickly slid into passive defensiveness.

If I had a do-over, Brittany would calmly explain that the room might not reach Sharon's preferred temperature and suggest the later class if that's what she needed. But instead, my ego swooped in. And I wasn't alone—everyone else's ego did the same, ushering us straight into The Drama Triangle.

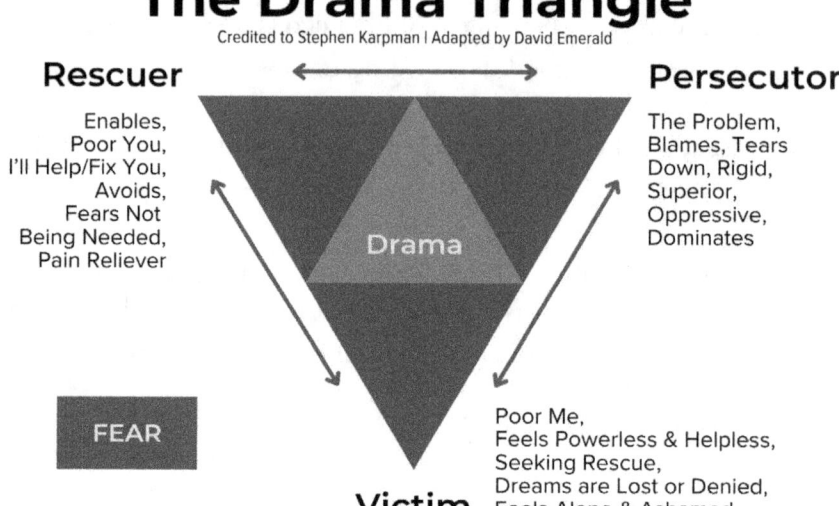

The Drama Triangle

Credited to Stephen Karpman | Adapted by David Emerald

Rescuer ⟷ **Persecutor**

Enables,
Poor You,
I'll Help/Fix You,
Avoids,
Fears Not
Being Needed,
Pain Reliever

The Problem,
Blames, Tears
Down, Rigid,
Superior,
Oppressive,
Dominates

Drama

FEAR

Poor Me,
Feels Powerless & Helpless,
Seeking Rescue,
Dreams are Lost or Denied,
Feels Alone & Ashamed

Victim

The Dreaded Drama Triangle

In the 1960s, psychologist Stephen Karpman introduced The Drama Triangle, a model that highlights the unconscious roles we often slip into during conflict: the victim, the persecutor, and the rescuer. These roles can create a cycle of negative emotions and behaviors, not just with others, but also how we relate to ourselves.

While Karpman didn't specifically use the term "ego self," many psychologists and therapists have since connected The Drama Triangle to ego-driven behaviors. These roles are often defense mechanisms our ego self uses to manage stress, protect us from vulnerability, or assert control in conflict situations—whether we're aware of it or not.

I've learned a ton about this work through a leadership training organization called The Conscious Leadership Group. I love filtering their work through the lens of yoga and the ego. Seeing how the ego self plays into the drama dynamics can offer deeper insight into how we show up in conflict and help us break free from the cycle of drama.

The Three Drama Triangle Roles

Whenever I find myself in a situation where I don't feel at peace or empowered, it's a strong indication that I'm playing one of the three roles in The Drama Triangle. And by "I'm playing," I mean Brandi has taken the lead and is acting from either a victim mindset, persecutor mindset, or rescuer mindset.

Victim Mindset

First, let's be clear: The "victim" in The Drama Triangle is different from actually being victimized by real harm—whether physical, mental, or emotional. In the triangle, the "victim" role comes from a place of perceived powerlessness, where life's normal challenges feel overwhelming and unchangeable. A "victim" believes that nothing they do will make a difference and waits for someone or something to save them. They seek sympathy and validation, often feeling stuck or helpless.

Some ego statements that are clues that I'm in a "victim" mindset might be:

- "I don't have enough time."
- "There's nothing I can do."
- "It's too hard."

- "It's all on me."
- "I have to."
- "It's not fair."

This mindset can feel oddly comforting because it absolves us of responsibility. When we feel powerless, there's no need to make things better, and that alone provides temporary relief.

But here's the dance: When I'm sick, tired, or facing a challenge, it's up to my higher self to acknowledge, *Yes, I feel bad, sad, or exhausted, and it makes sense that I do,* without letting Brandi take over with her familiar cry of, *Woe is me! It's too hard.* It's a delicate balance between honoring the discomfort and not slipping into the "victim" role.

Persecutor Mindset

On the flip side, when Brandi shifts focus to blame—whether it's directed at myself or others—it's a sign I'm playing the "persecutor." The persecutor thrives on being right and finding fault, whether through aggression or passive-aggression. This role gives the illusion of control by zeroing in on problems. Creativity and solutions are often absent because the persecutor already has the answer.

When Brandi is in persecutor mode, it might sound, or feel, like the following:

Ego persecutor statements when blaming others:

- "It's all your fault."
- "You're doing it wrong."
- "You should know better."

Ego persecutor statements when blaming oneself:

- "I'm so stupid."
- "I should know better."
- "I don't care."

Persecutors fixate on the problem to avoid feeling insecure, and while this role offers a sense of control, it's often a destructive and limiting form of control.

Yes, life presents its challenges, and my higher self can see the facts, feel the frustration or anger, and make healthy requests for change. In doing so, I'm able to move situations toward what I want, rather than staying trapped in the drama of blame and judgment where I stay focused on the problem.

Rescuer Mindset

Lastly, there's the "rescuer." When Brandi feels an overwhelming need to alleviate someone's suffering—whether it's my own or someone else's—she grabs her cape and swoops in to save the day. The rescuer wants to fix everything, even when no one has asked for help. But by stepping in, the rescuer often enables the victim's dependency, fueling the cycle of dysfunction.

Ego rescuer statements sound like:

- "I can do it."
- "Poor you. I can help."
- "You've got this!"
- "Let me fix it."
- "Where's the chocolate (wine, ice cream, TV remote, etc.)?"

While well intentioned, the rescuer is really just avoiding their own discomfort by focusing on someone else's. It's sneaky because it feels good. After all, the rescuer is "helping," right? But in reality, they're just keeping the drama alive by saving, rather than supporting.

When the higher self is in charge, the approach is very different. Instead of jumping into rescue mode, the higher self sees the person (or oneself) as capable and offers support from a place of strength. The higher self might say, "It's okay to feel everything, even sadness, anger, or frustration. Let me know if you need my support—I know you've got this."

The Sharon Drama, Explained

Now that you've met the three main characters in The Drama Triangle, let's take a closer look at how the different roles played out during the yoga class with Sharon. With the group's collective ego selves in agreement, it was easy to label Sharon as the obvious "persecutor." From the moment she demanded the room's temperature to be adjusted, it seemed like she was the one pointing fingers and asserting blame.

But if we flip the perspective, it could be that Sharon saw me and my assistant as the "persecutors." Maybe in her mind, we weren't maintaining the temperature properly, and that could have felt like a personal attack on her experience. She wanted things a certain way, and when those expectations weren't met, we became the ones at fault.

Janet and Brandi, on the other hand, immediately stepped into the "rescuer" role, trying to soothe Sharon by reassuring her, "It's going to be okay. You'll sweat plenty!"—even though we couldn't have known if that would be. Then, when Brandi wanted validation from the student and asked, "You get sweaty in this class, don't you?" she subtly slipped into the "victim" role. She was looking for the student to step in as her "rescuer" and save her from the uncomfortable interaction with Sharon.

And the student's ego was more than happy to oblige. They leaped into action, enthusiastically confirming, "Yes, I definitely sweat!"—playing the part of "rescuer" to make Brandi feel supported.

Meanwhile, across the room, some of the students' ego selves were in full judgment mode. They silently took on the "persecutor" role, wondering, *Who does Sharon think she is?* Others stood by, wishing they could do something to smooth things over, subtly stepping into the "rescuer" role as well.

During the class itself, Brandi continued to dance between roles. At one point, she switched back to the "victim" when she asked the class, "Is anyone getting hot yet?" She was seeking reassurance from the students, hoping to be rescued once again. And, as expected, the students' ego selves dutifully obliged, trying to rescue their teacher with responses like, "Yes, we're definitely feeling it!" Except, of course, Sharon wasn't having it. She held strong in what felt to Brandi like the "persecutor" role with her defiant, "NO!"

After class, the dynamic continued. When Janet passive-aggressively wished Sharon a good day, she shifted from rescuer to persecutor herself. It was a subtle but sharp jab cloaked in pleasantries—a way for her ego to feel some control over the situation.

This is what role-switching looks like. In the same scenario, we can move between victim, persecutor, and rescuer roles without even realizing it. Our egos are constantly adapting and reacting, and it's easy to see how drama can unfold when everyone is playing a part.

Role Switching

With all of that said, Brittany is the only person in the story I can actually control; so I've found it helpful to use this tool to reflect on how I'm personally acting out the roles of victim, persecutor, or rescuer. Brandi, the talented actress she is, can often play all three roles in a matter of minutes, shifting from one to another as she navigates a situation.

To illustrate this, let's dive into a single-person, three-act play where Brandi takes the stage in a coworking scenario from a few years ago:

Act One: Brandi begins the scene in full victim mode. She's frustrated by a coworker who isn't seeing things my way, and you can hear her inner monologue echoing through the room: *There's nothing I can do to have him see things differently.* Her helplessness sets the tone as she slumps into the role, convinced no amount of effort will change the situation.

Act Two: Without missing a beat, she shifts gears and takes on the persecutor role. Frustration bubbles up as she wonders, *Why would he even say something like that? He should know better.* Now, instead of feeling powerless, Brandi is on the attack. She's blaming him for the conflict and solidifying her position as the "right" one. The energy is sharp, and the blame game is in full swing.

Act Three: In an effort to soothe the discomfort she's feeling, Brandi takes on the rescuer role—except this time, she's rescuing herself. She reassures with, *I've got this. I'll be fine no matter what.* It might seem like a positive affirmation on the surface, but the truth is, Brandi is just trying to escape the situation, brushing it off without truly resolving anything. She's not acting from a place of grounded confidence, but from an anxious need to end the discomfort.

In this three-act play, we see how quickly Brandi can switch roles depending on how she's feeling at the moment. In a matter of minutes, she's gone from victim to persecutor to rescuer, cycling through The Drama Triangle without even realizing it.

Now, if you're like Brandi and default to the rescuer role, you might wonder what could be wrong with reassuring yourself: "I've got this. I'll be fine no matter what." After all, isn't that a positive statement?

The key difference is the origin of that statement. When spoken with confidence and creativity, it's empowering. It's an acknowledgment that I'm capable and resourceful enough to navigate the challenge. But when it's a reaction—an attempt to avoid discomfort or brush off the conflict without addressing it—it's a sign I'm stuck in the rescuer role in The Drama Triangle. I'm trying to erase uncomfortable feelings, rather than working through them.

If that distinction doesn't fully make sense yet, don't worry—it will likely become clearer as we explore The Empowerment Dynamic later in the chapter. First, let's see how we invite others to jump in the mud—the drama—with us.

What's mud got to do with it?

When things get sticky, Brandi has a way of inviting others to jump into the mud with her, pulling them into the roles of The Drama Triangle. Sometimes, she'll invite a friend to rescue her, because what's better than having someone swoop in to save the day? It feels like a win-win.

Win #1: As the victim, Brandi gets to feel valued because her friend wants to save her.

Win #2: The friend feels valued because they get to be the rescuer and make Brandi feel better. Both walk away with a sense of validation, even though they're just splashing around in the drama.

Other times, Brandi doesn't need saving; she wants someone to stand beside her and throw some mud. She'll find a friend to persecute alongside her: "You're right, Brandi! He's awful. I can't believe someone would even say that!" Suddenly, there's a little drama party happening, where being "right" becomes the prize, and I get the dopamine hit— the "cookie." Sure, the situation is messy, but the validation from a friend makes it feel like a justified, feel-good experience.

Things and Events can also Persecute or Rescue Us

It's not just people who pull us into these roles—life itself can play the part. Events like getting sick, living through a pandemic, or saying goodbye to someone you love can easily pull you into the victim role. Here, the persecutor is the situation itself—something beyond your control that leaves you feeling helpless, frustrated, or defeated. And when that happens, Brandi will start looking for a rescuer. But instead of a person, it might be food, drink, scrolling social media, or binge-watching TV shows—anything that numbs the discomfort and makes her feel saved from the moment.

Why Are We Drawn to the Drama like a Moth to Flame?

From her high horse, Brandi can look around and point out all the victims, persecutors, and rescuers in the room—never realizing that she's the star of all three roles in her own drama. It's so much easier to see others stuck in The Drama Triangle than it is to see yourself there. After all, it's more comfortable to blindly play the part than admit you're on stage at all.

Drawing from insights I've learned from The Conscious Leadership Group, I see that it's no wonder we resist seeing ourselves in the drama—Brandi has plenty of reasons to stay stuck there. Sometimes, it feels easier to **wait for someone else to swoop in and save** her, rather than face the discomfort of dealing with things on her own. Taking responsibility can feel daunting, and if she waits long enough, maybe someone will rescue her from it all.

Other times, it's easier to **shift the blame onto someone or something else**. Brandi loves pointing fingers because, if someone else is at fault, she doesn't have to take a hard look at her own role in the situation. She's also pretty skilled at **comparing herself to others**—at least my situation isn't as bad as theirs, she thinks, distracting herself from the fact that her own struggles need attention. It's a **temporary relief**, but it doesn't change anything.

Then there's that irresistible dopamine hit when Brandi gets **to be right**. She clings to the feeling of superiority—also known as **"not being wrong"**—because being right gives her a sense of power, no matter how insignificant the situation is. It's like a game she plays, reinforcing the idea that if she's right, everything is under control.

Sometimes, Brandi indulges in gossip or mental storytelling. It starts out innocently, but soon enough, it becomes her default way of avoiding uncomfortable emotions. Whether it's external gossip or internal drama playing out in her head, it keeps her **entertained and distracted** from the real issues at hand—she can just keep spinning the story.

There's also that sneaky **rush of energy** she gets when she plays the roles of persecutor or rescuer. These roles give her a strange **sense of control**—blaming someone else or swooping in to save the day. Even playing the victim has its perks, because sooner or later, someone will come to her rescue. In those moments, it's easy to get caught up in the drama because, for a brief time, it feels good.

But underneath it all, Brandi is **avoiding her raw emotions** bubbling up inside. She doesn't want to face the sadness, frustration, or anger below the surface. If she acknowledges those feelings, she might have to admit she's part of the problem—or even the whole problem— so she's **avoiding stepping into the unknown**. And that feels much scarier than staying stuck in the familiar comfort of drama.

Avoiding responsibility lets Brandi continue the cycle, because owning her role would mean needing to take action and make changes, and sometimes that feels too hard or too scary to face.

Before we move out of the drama, we have to first truly admit where we are in the drama. So very quickly and without shame, try the next practice, and then we'll shift into Presence and The Empowerment Dynamic.

Practice #9: What Does Your Ego Tend to Say in Drama?

In your journal or the workbook:

1. **Make a list of things you tend to hear yourself say when you aren't feeling peaceful in a situation.** You could pull from your journaling in Chapter 3 on ego statements or reference earlier pages in this chapter for clues.

   Examples: "I don't have enough time." "There's nothing I can do." "It's too hard." "It's all on me; I have to." "It's not fair." "It's all your fault." "I'm so stupid." "You're doing it wrong." "You should know better." "I don't care." "I can do it." "Poor you. I can help." "You can do it!" "I've got this." "Let's just have fun." "I'll make it right."

2. **Make three columns in your journal or three headings in your journaling app. Title the first column "Victim," the second column "Persecutor," and the third column "Rescuer."** Put your ego statements under The Drama Triangle roles they match.

3. **After looking at the things you say, which role(s) in The Drama Triangle do you default play?** Use caution here:

   ○ If you tend to play the Victim or Rescuer, you may drift further into the drama because you feel shame about being in the drama.

   ○ If you tend to play the Persecutor, you may drift further as you defend or try to be logical about it.

   ○ Be gentle with yourself—it can get pretty sad and funny at times to witness the shame/should spirals.

Now that you see the roles you tend to play in the drama of life, it's time to recognize how your higher self can take the lead outside of drama.

Presence

When our higher selves are leading, we move into a state of **Presence**, where we're able to navigate life's challenges with grace, clarity, and calm. In Presence, instead of reacting from a place of fear or defensiveness, we tap into **deeper awareness**. Imagine facing a tough conversation at work. Instead of jumping to blame or shrinking from conflict, your higher self is curious—willing to learn from the experience. You find yourself **open to possibilities** rather than being stuck in a right-versus-wrong mentality.

In this state, you're not afraid to **laugh at yourself**, even in awkward or stressful moments. For example, if you make a mistake during a presentation, instead of spiraling into embarrassment, you can smile and say, "Well, that didn't go as planned!" Presence allows you to see your **missteps as opportunities** rather than failures.

When you're operating from Presence, you **take responsibility for your part** in situations without letting shame take over. Let's say you and a friend have a disagreement. Instead of placing blame, your higher self reflects, "What was my role in this, and how can I communicate more clearly next time?" **You see others as allies**, not enemies, willing to work together to resolve issues.

Presence also invites **honesty**. Rather than hiding behind defensiveness or masking your true feelings, you're able to **speak unarguably** about what's happening with you. Speaking unarguably means speaking from what you are seeing, hearing, tasting, smelling, feeling, imagining. Your experience can't be challenged because it is your experience and not someone else's. For example, if you're feeling overwhelmed, instead of pretending everything is fine, you might say, "I'm feeling really stressed right now and could use some space to gather my thoughts." This kind of **communication fosters connection and understanding**, both with yourself and others inside and outside of conflict.

In Presence, emotions are no longer something to resist or control. You **allow yourself to feel fully**—whether it's joy, sadness, or frustration—without pushing those feelings away. If you feel anger rising, instead of snapping at someone or bottling it up, you pause, breathe deeply, and acknowledge, "I'm feeling really angry right now. Let me take a moment before I respond." The **ability to breathe and move with ease** becomes a natural part of navigating challenges, allowing you to stay grounded no matter what comes your way.

TED* (*The Empowerment Dynamic)®

Now that we've explored the state of Presence and how it allows us to respond with clarity rather than react out of fear, let's bring it back to Karpman's Drama Triangle for just a moment. His model shows us how easily we slip into playing the roles of victim, persecutor, or rescuer when our ego selves take over. These roles create unhealthy patterns that trap us in cycles of conflict and drama. But once we can see ourselves caught in this triangle, we can begin to break free.

So how do we escape this cycle? You've already learned a few tools as baby steps out of the drama in the previous chapters, and we will build on those with The Empowerment Dynamic. It's one of my absolute favorite tools that was created by David Emerald and Donna Zajonc in the early 2000s. While Karpman's model helps us identify when we're stuck in drama, Emerald and Zajonc's Empowerment Dynamic gives us a road map for moving toward healthier, more constructive ways of interacting with ourselves and others.

Before diving into how The Empowerment Dynamic works, let's try a simple exercise (one I learned from a workshop with David Emerald) to illustrate the concept of switching perspectives. Set your book or device down and cross your arms.

Look down and notice which arm is on the outside—your right or your left. Say to yourself, "right" or "left," depending on what you see, so you're clear on which it is. Now, switch the cross so the other arm is on the outside.

It may have been easy or somewhat awkward, but what's important is that you notice two things: you have a default way of doing things, and you have the ability to switch. Just like this simple action, we can learn to switch from playing roles in The Drama Triangle to operating from more empowered positions.

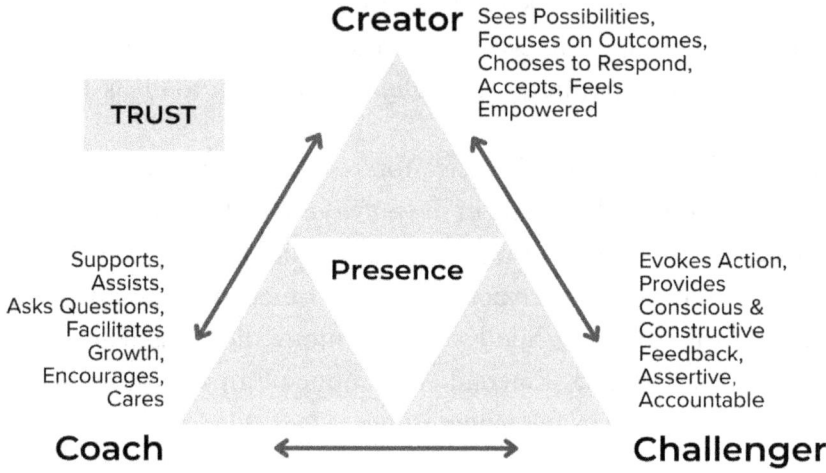

The Empowerment Dynamic®

Credited to David Emerald and Donna Zajonc | Adapted with Permission
www.brittanyhopkins.com/ted

Creator Sees Possibilities, Focuses on Outcomes, Chooses to Respond, Accepts, Feels Empowered

TRUST

Supports, Assists, Asks Questions, Facilitates Growth, Encourages, Cares

Presence

Evokes Action, Provides Conscious & Constructive Feedback, Assertive, Accountable

Coach ⟷ **Challenger**

In The Empowerment Dynamic, the roles we play shift from disempowerment to empowerment. Instead of staying stuck in the victim role, we move into the position of the creator. Persecutors become challengers, and rescuers transform into coaches. This model beautifully highlights the contrast between when I let Brandi take the wheel—reacting out of anxiety, frustration, or fear—and when I, as my higher self, am firmly in the driver's seat, with Brandi buckled up next to me, hands in her lap.

When Brandi's in control, everything feels like a crisis. She thrives on overthinking and reacting to every little thing, convinced the world is against her. It's as if Brandi is gripping the wheel too tight, trying to steer through life's twists and turns by bracing for impact. But when

I'm leading from my higher self, I can see that I don't have to react to every obstacle like it's a life-or-death situation. Instead, I become the creator, someone who sees opportunities where Brandi only sees problems. The road ahead may still be bumpy, but I can navigate it calmly and with a sense of purpose, knowing that while I may not be able to control a situation, as my higher self, I do have control over how I respond.

Similarly, when Brandi steps into the role of persecutor, she's quick to judge and blame, pointing fingers at others or herself. It's like being stuck in traffic, honking the horn and yelling at other drivers, but getting nowhere. But when my higher self shifts into the role of the challenger, there's a shift in perspective. Instead of attacking or blaming, I'm able to pose thoughtful questions, both to myself and others, that encourage growth and problem-solving. The obstacles on the road aren't roadblocks; they're opportunities to rise to the occasion.

Then there's Brandi's default rescuer mode. When she feels uncomfortable, she rushes in to fix things, whether or not anyone has asked for her help. It's like trying to change the tire on someone else's car when yours still has a flat. In contrast, when I step into the role of the coach, I can offer support and guidance without taking over. I see the other person as capable and strong, just as I see myself. Instead of swooping in to solve the problem, I support them finding their own way, empowering both of us in the process.

The Empowerment Dynamic gives us a clear path to follow—a way to shift from reactivity to conscious, intentional action. Whether we're confronting a challenge or offering support, we have the choice to drive as our higher self, keeping our ego safely in the passenger seat.

Let's dive deeper into each of The Empowerment Dynamic roles, starting with how to be a creator in our lives.

"Life doesn't happen to you, it happens for you." —Tony Robbins

Creators

It's important to understand that being a creator doesn't mean life becomes free of challenges. The same day-to-day struggles, like navigating illness, enduring a pandemic, or dealing with the loss of a loved one, still come our way. The difference is in how creators respond to these events.

When we're operating from the creator role (our higher self) we don't resist what life throws at us the way victims (our egos in The Drama Triangle) do.

When our egos are playing the role of victim, we feel like *life is happening to us,* and we often push back against circumstances, convinced we're powerless. This resistance, born from ego, keeps us stuck in a cycle of suffering and helplessness.

As creators, on the other hand, we move with the flow of life and feel like *life is happening for us,* even if it's hard. Creators acknowledge challenges but don't get swept away by them.

Imagine standing in a river—drama triangle victims fight against the current, paddling upstream, while creators understand that the current is part of the journey. Creators use the energy of the water to guide them forward, rather than trying to resist the inevitable.

Victim Brandi vs. Creator Brittany

When Brandi is in victim mode, she feels powerless. She believes that life is happening to her, leaving her stuck in a cycle of frustration and helplessness. But when I'm operating as Brittany, a creator, I feel powerful.

> Creators recognize that while we may not control every situation, we *can* control how we respond.

Brandi often focuses on scarcity, seeing only what's missing or lacking in life. Whether it's time, money, or love, she's consumed by a sense of "not enough." Brittany, on the other hand, taps into possibilities. As a creator, I ask, "What could happen if I stay open?" and suddenly, doors that seemed closed before start to crack open.

Another key difference between the two mindsets is how they handle emotions. Brandi, the victim, resists both the small and big feelings, letting them build up and overtake her. She tries to avoid discomfort at all costs, which only makes her feel more stuck. Brittany, the creator, allows those same emotions to flow through her, knowing they're temporary and part of the human experience.

> When we allow ourselves to feel fully, we create space for growth and healing.

Brandi, in victim mode, focuses on the problem—what's wrong, what's not working, what feels impossible. Brittany, the creator, focuses on the desired outcome. Instead of dwelling on what I don't want, I think about what I do want and take steps, no matter how small, to move toward that vision.

Brandi clings to her beliefs, defending them even when they no longer serve her. It's a stuck mindset, one that keeps her in repeating cycles. But Brittany, as a creator, questions those beliefs.

> Creators are open to learning and evolving, and ask, "Is this belief really true? Is this belief helping me?" This openness allows them to break free from limitations.

Operating from the victim mindset, Brandi moves through life feeling like she "should" do this or that—she's bound by expectations and obligations. Brittany, the creator, approaches life with curiosity and passion.

> Creators follow what excites them, what lights them up, instead of what they feel obligated to do.

One of the biggest shifts between victim and creator is how they see choices. Brandi feels boxed in, unable to see a way out—everything feels limited. Brittany sees possibilities.

> When in creator mode, we know that we always have choices, even in the most challenging situations.

Finally, Brandi often feels "less than" others, comparing herself and coming up short. Brittany knows that we're all equals.

> Creators don't need to measure themselves against others; instead, they can recognize their worth, alongside everyone else's.

I know I'm fully in creator mode when I can breathe deeply and move through life with ease. In this space, I'm taking conscious, small steps toward what I want to create, rather than unconsciously running away from what I don't want.

When life gets "wonky"—whether it's my kid getting sick and needing to stay home from school or someone denting my car in a parking lot without leaving a note—I practice noticing the drama as it bubbles up. I might swirl in The Drama Triangle for a minute (or an hour), but eventually, I make my way back into the creator mindset, where I can respond with clarity and intention.

After embracing the creator mindset, the next step in The Empowerment Dynamic is to explore how we can shift from being a persecutor to becoming a challenger. This transformation is a key part of how we relate to others and ourselves when we face conflict or difficult situations.

> *"The greatest challenge to any thinker is stating the problem in a way that will allow a solution."* —BERTRAND RUSSELL

Challengers

One of the main differences between an ego persecutor and a higher self challenger is in how they view others.

A persecutor tends to see the other person as a problem, someone to be blamed or corrected, while a challenger sees them as a creator—capable and empowered to make their own choices.

A challenger is willing to provide feedback, even if it's difficult, but does so from a place of compassion and authenticity. This may look like a compassionate confrontation, where the goal is to invite the other person into alignment, not to punish or shame them.

> The key to being a challenger is
> knowing when to back off.

If the other person isn't receptive to the feedback, the challenger doesn't push harder. If they were to keep pushing when the other person isn't receptive, they would then ultimately drift back down into the persecutor role of The Drama Triangle. Instead, they recognize that if the person is stuck in a victim mindset, they may not be ready to receive feedback. This is where we need to stay in creator mode and avoid slipping into the drama ourselves.

> It's important to remember: We don't get
> to decide how we're received by others.

If someone is operating from a victim mindset, they may perceive you as a persecutor, no matter how well intentioned your feedback is. If your ego steps in and starts seeing them as a victim, you've drifted into the drama with them. In many instances, whether people realize it or not, they're choosing the victim mindset.

As a challenger, the key is to detach from your own beliefs and judgments, stay in the creator role, and continue seeing the other person as a creator too—someone with choices and the power to act.

Persecutor Brandi vs. Challenger Brittany

When Brandi steps into the persecutor role, she wants others to feel bad because they're wrong. (And she's right.) Whether it's through judgment, blame, or criticism, she gets stuck in self-righteousness. But when Brittany steps into the challenger role, I apply kind, loving pressure to empower others to find alignment.

> The goal isn't to punish, but to guide,
> offering feedback that invites others to
> step up without feeling belittled.

Brandi, the persecutor, gets stuck in patterns of unfiltered anger or frustration, replaying what went wrong over and over. But Brittany is comfortable feeling authentic emotions like anger or frustration—I don't ruminate with or avoid these feelings.

> As a challenger, we use feelings as
> fuel to clarify our desires and take
> actions that move things forward.

The ego clings tightly to beliefs and behaviors, defending them even when they're no longer useful. As a persecutor, Brandi resists letting go in conflict because she believes it would make her weak or bad. In contrast, Brittany, the challenger, is willing to release outdated beliefs and behaviors, knowing they're no longer of service.

> Leading as challengers, we're open
> to learning and growing, even if it
> means admitting we're wrong.

While Brandi thinks certain things *should* have never happened—staying stuck in regret or judgment, Brittany, as a challenger, is committed to learning from every experience, even the hard ones.

Challengers accept the past and move
forward with a deeper understanding of
how to make better choices in the future.

When Brandi gets stuck in reaction mode, she repeats old patterns without pausing to think that she's persecuting—like the time I snapped at Adam when I was hungry and tired, assuming he didn't care as much as I did about prepping for the party. But Brittany steps into action, inviting others to do the same. Even if I'm hungry and tired, I can acknowledge that and consciously choose my next steps, looking for a way to move forward constructively.

While Brandi is quick to judge what others do as right or wrong—like when I felt frustrated after someone cut me off in traffic—Brittany is willing to question herself, staying open to the possibility that I don't know everything about the other person's life. Maybe they're rushing to the hospital or dealing with an emergency. This openness is key to being a challenger—it's what allows me to challenge others with compassion rather than judgment.

Finally, Brandi is always on the lookout for someone or something to blame. Whether it's a person, a circumstance, or even herself, she deflects responsibility—like when I blamed the kids being home for my inability to get the house cleaned. Brittany, the challenger, takes responsibility where necessary, even if it's difficult. Instead of blaming Isaac and Vinni for interrupting, I pause, take a breath, and own the fact that I can either set clearer boundaries or reassess my expectations for what can be accomplished with two kiddos present.

Challengers understand that real growth
comes from owning their part in every
situation, not from shifting blame elsewhere.

After understanding the role of the challenger, it's time to explore the final piece of The Empowerment Dynamic: the coach. While the challenger pushes us toward growth by confronting our assumptions and actions, the coach guides and supports us, offering the resources and space to find our own path forward.

> *"The job of a coach is to make oneself unnecessary."* —UNKNOWN

Coaches

The key difference between an ego rescuer and a higher self coach is how they view the other person. A rescuer sees someone as powerless, needing to be saved, while a coach sees the other person as a creator—someone with the potential to learn and grow from their experiences.

A coach understands that true empowerment doesn't come from offering quick fixes or temporary relief, as a rescuer does. Instead, they hold space for others to face their own challenges, even if it means allowing them to experience temporary discomfort. This discomfort is often necessary for future growth.

Coaches know that lasting empowerment
requires patience, trust, and the willingness
to see others as equal and capable.

While both challengers and coaches support the creator mindset in
The Empowerment Dynamic, their approaches differ. Higher self
challengers focus on providing short-term pressure to spark growth,
often through direct feedback and confrontation. In contrast, higher
self coaches take a longer-term approach, offering guidance, support,
and resources that allow the creator to make their own decisions and
chart their own course over time.

Rescuer Brandi vs. Coach Brittany

When Brandi takes on the rescuer role, she sees herself as better or more
capable than others, believing that they lack the ability to handle things
on their own. She swoops in to solve their problems, reinforcing their
dependence on her. But Brittany, the coach, sees everyone as equals.

The coach knows that others have the ability
to learn and grow, even if it means letting
them face challenges on their own.

Brandi validates others' victim stories, fostering their reliance on her
"support" to feel better. She thrives on being the one to make things
right and sees people's lives as problems to be solved. She is quick
to tell others what to do, convinced that they can't figure it out on

their own. Brittany trusts that others will find the right answers for themselves, offering support only when needed or asked.

> A coach encourages others to see their own power and abilities. Rather than providing the solution, coaches ask questions that support others in finding their *own* way forward.

Brandi often falls into repetitive patterns of drama, solving the same problems over and over again for herself and others. Brittany opens the door to new ways of thinking and doing, even if those new ways feel uncomfortable or scary at first.

> Coaches see challenges as opportunities for growth—not obstacles to be removed.

Rescuer Brandi tends to live in the past, using it to try and control what happens in the future. She believes that if she can just fix things now, everything will be okay later. Coach Brittany lives in the present. She invites others to create something new, right here and now, rather than obsessing over what has already happened.

As a rescuer, Brandi takes on responsibilities that aren't hers, believing that others can't handle them. Brittany, the coach, supports others in taking responsibility for their own lives.

> Coaches empower others to step up and own their choices.

Finally, Brandi looks for quick and easy fixes that provide temporary relief, but they rarely last. Brittany, the coach, is focused on creating lasting results.

Coaches know that true growth
takes time and patience.

By embracing the coach mindset, we move away from the patterns of fixing and rescuing and step into a more supportive, empowering role. This not only helps others grow but allows us to live more fully in alignment with our higher selves.

Putting it Together

Imagine a line that separates two ways of operating in the world. Above the line, we're empowered—taking responsibility for our actions, viewing challenges as opportunities for growth, and interacting as our higher self. Below the line, we're reactive, driven by our ego self, feeling powerless, defensive, or blaming others for our circumstances.

The Drama Triangle exists below the line. When we're in this space, we're stuck in the roles of victim, persecutor, or rescuer, operating from our ego self, reacting to situations rather than responding consciously. In this state, we're often more concerned with being right, protecting ourselves, or avoiding discomfort. It's a place where we might feel powerless, where life is happening to us rather than through us.

Above the line is The Empowerment Dynamic, where we step into the roles of creator, challenger, or coach. Here, we engage with life from our higher self, taking proactive steps to shape our experience, facing challenges with curiosity and courage, and offering support in ways that empower others rather than enable them.

Above the line, life is not happening
to us—it's happening *through* us.

Understanding where you exist in relation to this line—whether you drift and you're caught in the drama below or act from a place of empowerment above—can help you recognize when it's time to shift your perspective. By making the conscious decision to step into your higher self, you can respond to life's challenges with greater clarity, compassion, and confidence.

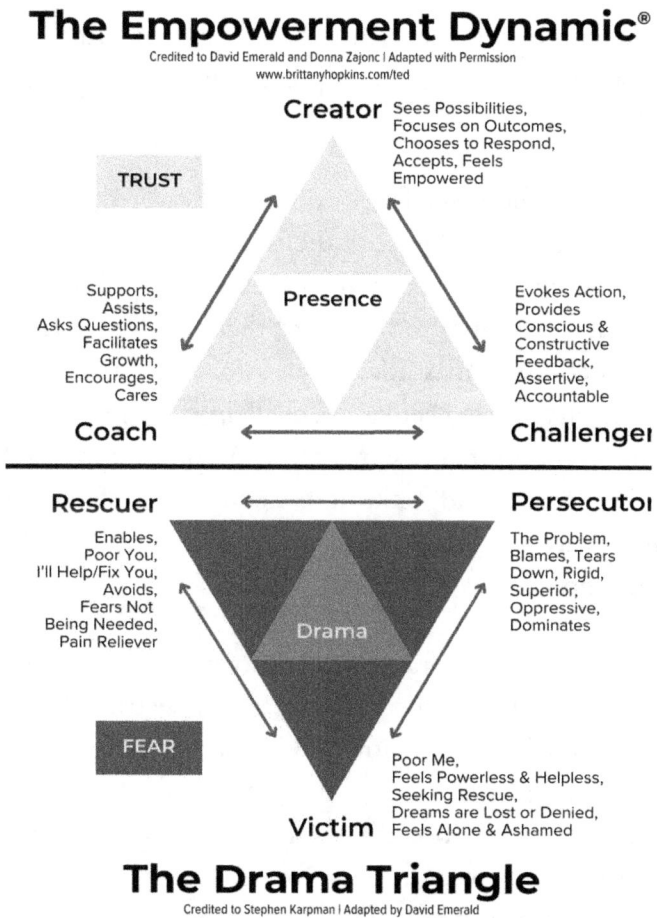

Let's look at the drifts and shifts in a real-life scenario. Looking back on the experience with Sharon in class, we can now see how I drifted below the line into The Drama Triangle and shifted back up above the line into The Empowerment Dynamic, before, during, and after class.

The Empowerment Dynamic and Sharon

At the start of class, I consciously chose to step into The Empowerment Dynamic. I planted my feet, asked the class to join me in a deep breath, and introduced the theme for the practice. In that moment, I was operating as a creator, fully present and focused on setting an empowering tone for the class.

However, during the first fifteen minutes, I wavered between Brandi and Brittany. I bounced between the roles of victim, persecutor, and rescuer as Brandi tried to take control. Yet, when I stood tall, breathed deeply with my students, and watched them move, I was back in the creator mindset. I saw my students as creators, each making the choice to be on their mats, and I spoke as a challenger, giving direct feedback on alignment in different instances. As coach, I empowered them to listen to their bodies and make adjustments as they needed through their practice, trusting they knew what was best for their bodies and minds from moment to moment.

There were times where Brandi pulled me back down to The Drama Triangle. When I asked the class, "Are you getting hot yet?" and Sharon responded loudly with "NO," it was a clear moment of Brandi's victim and persecutor energy clashing. But, in seeing how absurd the situation had become, I shifted back up above the line with my higher self. I took responsibility for my part in the drama, released the need to be right, and settled into the creator mindset for the rest of the class. I'll talk more about how I harness Brandi for good in my life later in the book, but for now, know that I pulled from Brandi's ability to bring levity when the mood seemed overly serious. I also listened when she reminded me that I have a ton of experience under my belt, which allowed the class to continue to flow through the hiccups.

After class, when Janie told me about her passive-aggressive "Have a great day, Sharon!" moment, I stepped into the challenger role with compassion. I asked her to reflect on her motivation, guiding her to recognize her slip into the persecutor role. She took the challenge with grace, stepping into the creator role herself, acknowledging her behavior with clarity and humor.

With the trainees, I acted as a coach, seeing them as creators capable of reflecting on their participation in the drama. The trainee who tried to "rescue" me by claiming she always sweated in my classes was quick to laugh at herself after class, showing that she, too, recognized her shift into the rescuer role.

The group in the lobby, who witnessed Sharon's dramatic entrance and exit, also became creators. They took responsibility for their initial judgmental reactions and acknowledged their desire to "rescue" me by enthusiastically agreeing that the room was hot when I asked.

Ultimately, I remained in the creator role by finding gratitude for Sharon's presence. Her intensity provided a perfect real-time scenario for me and the trainees to observe how easily we all slip into The Drama Triangle. It allowed me to point out moments where I was below the line in drama, creating a powerful learning opportunity for everyone.

Even after that weekend, Sharon became a lighthearted reference point for us. Our egos sometimes joked about whether she would return, and in those moments, we drifted below the line for some shared laughs about how quickly and easily we could go there. After all, entertainment is one of the reasons many choose to stay in the drama of life. But our higher selves would bring us back up above the line with gratitude for the lessons Sharon brought us about how we unconsciously drift into drama and can intentionally shift into empowerment.

To support you in shifting above the line, I have a series of journaling practices that help lift you out of the drama and into empowerment.

Tools for Making the Shift Happen

The upcoming practices are designed to support you in the present moment, where countless possibilities exist. Whether you choose to do them alone in a journal or with a trusted person, both methods are effective. Personally, I enjoy doing these with a friend, but journaling works just as well.

If you decide to practice with someone else, I have a request: Invite them to refrain from jumping into the mud with you. Ask them to listen generously, which means they're fully present and hearing what you're saying without formulating a response or jumping in with their own stories. If they do respond, it should simply be to share what they heard you say, nothing more.

Practice #10 offers a lot of tools—nine, to be exact. It may be helpful to read through all of them first and then go back and work through them in your journal, or with a friend.

Before each practice, I share how I used it to work through a drama I had when I owned, and ran, a yoga studio, and then I invite you to try it out.

The Drama of a Bubbling Yoga Floor

In 2019, we'd finally completed a beautiful build-out of our new heated yoga room with infrared heating panels and state-of-the-art padded floor. Everything seemed perfect—until the floor started to bubble. I was overcome with frustration. When I reached out to the installation company, they admitted fault but insisted on closing the studio for a week to fix the issue.

I wasn't willing to close for an entire week because of their mistake. I suggested they fix the floor over Labor Day weekend to minimize the impact on my business, but they refused, saying their staff wasn't available. That's when I realized I was trapped in The Drama Triangle.

I was playing the roles of:

- **Victim:** Brandi felt like the situation was completely unfair. Thinking: *This isn't right. Why do we have to suffer because of their mistake?*
- **Persecutor:** Brandi turned the installation company into the enemy, thinking: *They're at fault. It's their responsibility to fix this on my terms.*
- **Rescuer:** Brandi called friends to vent, hoping they'd agree with me, saying, "Yes, you're right. The company is definitely wrong. They should fix the floor over Labor Day weekend."

The installation company became the "persecutor" in the story—they did a bad job with the floor and weren't willing to be flexible with the repair timing.

Now it's your turn. If at any point you start to feel overwhelmed, give yourself permission to take breaks. It's important to move through these practices at your own pace.

Practice #10.1: Identify Your Drama

In your journal, the free workbook, or with a friend:

1. **Take some time to reflect on a current situation in your life where you're not feeling at peace.** It could be related to work, a relationship, your health, or any other area that feels unsettled.

2. **Identify Your Role(s) in The Drama Triangle**

   a. **Are you taking on the role of the victim?**

   If so, what thoughts or statements are coming up that indicate you're in a "victim" mindset?

   Example: "This always happens to me," or "There's nothing I can do about it."

   b. **Are you playing the persecutor?**

   If so, what are you saying or thinking that places blame on others or the situation?

   Example: "They're the ones at fault," or "Why can't they just do their job right?" or "I should have known better."

   c. **Are you playing the rescuer?**

   If so, what actions or thoughts suggest you're stepping in to fix things for others, even when it's not your responsibility?

   Example: "I have to step in or everything will fall apart," or "It's my job to keep everyone happy," or "I'm fine. Everything's fine."

3. **Identify the Drama Triangle Roles of Others or Events**

   a. **Who do you see as the "victim" in this situation?**

   Why do you think they feel powerless or are acting from a place of helplessness?

   Example: "My coworker keeps saying they can't do anything right," or "She just doesn't have enough time."

   b. **Who, or what, do you view as the "persecutor"?'**

   Is it a person, event, or circumstance (such as an illness, financial stress, etc.) that you feel is causing harm or adding to the problem?

Example: "The pandemic ruined everything," or "This illness is the reason I can't move forward."

c. **Is there anyone or anything acting as the "rescuer" in the situation?**

This could be a person, an activity, or even a substance that's providing temporary relief.

Example: "I turn to food to comfort myself when things go wrong," or "They're constantly looking to their partner to fix the situation."

The Drama of a Bubbling Yoga Floor, Exaggerated

I remember vividly standing at the registration counter in the yoga studio lobby, ranting about the bubbling floor to two instructors. My arms were crossed, and my eyebrows were furrowed in deep frustration. I was pointing my finger, like I had been personally attacked by the flooring company. Brandi said things like, "Those JERKS need to take responsibility! THIS IS THEIR FAULT!"

I was nearly stomping my foot as I continued, "WHY SHOULD I have to make the sacrifice?! They need to fix it when I SAY SO!"

I was not the calm, peaceful yogi one would imagine a yoga studio owner to be—I was fully Brandi in all her glory—D-R-A-M-A-T-I-C!

From that exaggerated place, I was able to laugh out loud. Seeing the situation blown up like that made it easier to spot how I was fully locked into both the "victim" and "persecutor" roles. Inside the drama, I wasn't empowered to take any action, because I was so caught up in the emotion of the situation.

Now it's your turn. Write or say your situation as dramatically as possible, so you can fully identify The Drama Triangle roles you're playing.

Practice #10.2: Exaggerate Your Current Attitude

To get some clarity, it's time to have a little fun with this and dive into the drama with full force.

Take your current situation and exaggerate in a way that a theater teacher might coach someone to play a part bigger, better, and bolder—really go for it!

If you're talking it out with a friend, use dramatic gestures, intensify your voice, and don't be afraid to get over-the-top. If you are writing it out in your journal, bold or italicize your words. Make it big so you can see just how much drama is there.

The Drama of a Bubbling Yoga Floor, What if

If nothing changed about my situation, I would be left with a bubbled yoga studio floor indefinitely and I would continue to feel annoyed and frustrated every time I'd walk into the yoga studio.

If nothing changed about my situation, I would continue to feel powerless and continue to complain to the people in my life about the bubbled floor.

If nothing changed about my situation, people would probably tire of hearing me rant about the bubbled floor—potentially causing some relationships to deteriorate.

If nothing changed about my situation, I would probably get sick of hearing myself complain—causing my relationship with myself to deteriorate, too. None of the complaints would support forward motion in finding a solution to the bubbled floor.

You're invited to step into a powerful reflection with the "What if..." game. These next two questions came from a Baptiste Institute training I attended in 2018.

Practice #10.3: What if...

This exercise helps you explore the consequences of staying in the drama and imagine what your life would feel like if nothing changes.

Set a timer for **two minutes**.

Using the same situation from the previous practice where you weren't feeling at peace, answer the following questions, in writing or out loud, repeatedly until the timer goes off.

- **What if nothing changes in your situation? What would life look like and feel like? What would you be left with?**

Don't hold back—really let yourself explore what it would mean if things stayed exactly as they are, without any movement or resolution. This practice can be eye-opening as you get a sense of the stagnation or discomfort that could remain. It helps you see the cost of staying stuck in the drama and invites a shift toward more empowering actions.

Before we move on, try this: Don't change anything about how you're sitting or standing. Just notice your current posture. Take a deep breath in and exhale fully. Notice the depth of your breath and how it feels in your body without trying to change anything.

A Shortcut to Feeling Better

Simply changing your posture and breathing on purpose can make all the difference in arriving fully in the present. It's one of my favorite ways to shift out of drama without trying to argue with Brandi or convince her to change her perspective. If I'm feeling frustrated, sad, or tired, I can stand up tall, pull my shoulders back, and instantly, the shift begins.

Scientific research explains that this kind of physical and energetic shift works because of sensory feedback, neuromuscular activation, and spinal alignment. These signals tell your brain that you are in a strong, capable posture, which can positively influence both your body and mind.

Learning this was a lightbulb moment for me—it explained why I feel so good after a yoga class. Pose after pose, I'm lengthening my spine, opening my chest, and breathing deeply, often without needing to consciously change my thoughts.

In yoga, we're simply making shapes that allow the brain to release hormones that promote feelings of happiness, reduce stress, and create a sense of well-being.

The Drama of a Bubbling Yoga Floor, Posture Change

After overexaggerating the floor situation, I could see how Brandi was caught up in her comfort zone. I tried this posture practice. I uncrossed my arms, relaxed my hands down by my sides, pulled my shoulders back, and relaxed my neck. My posture became undefended. I didn't even have to tell myself to take a deep breath—it just happened naturally as my chest opened up. Then, I noticed how grounded I felt with my feet flat on the floor, and it led me into the next practice with clarity.

Now you try!

Practice #10.4: Drastically Change Your Posture and Breathe on Purpose

1. **If you're sitting, sit up tall and pull your shoulders back.** Even better, stand up tall with your shoulders back.

2. **Take a deep breath in and exhale fully.** Notice the difference in how deeply you can breathe.

3. **Bonus**: Set the book down, and take five more deep breaths while maintaining this posture.

Fun Facts About Heart Math

Before moving on, I want to tell you a little bit about the HeartMath Institute. This organization has done some fascinating research on how the heart, brain, and emotions are interconnected—specifically looking at the heart rate, the thalamus (the brain's message sorter), and the amygdala (the brain's emotional responder). Their findings explain how when these three parts of our body work together they affect our state of mind for better or for worse.

To put it simply:

- **When we feel frustrated**, our heart rate becomes erratic, which throws off the brain's ability to process clearly, creating circular, cloudy thinking.
- **When we feel grateful**, our heart rate steadies, which helps the brain function in a more coherent way, allowing for clearer thinking.

As wild as it sounds, a shortcut to clearer thinking is to practice gratitude.

The Drama of a Bubbling Yoga Floor, Gratitude

Before I stood tall and took deep breaths, I felt tight and constricted. Those feelings made sense because I was angry and stuck in a victim mindset. After physically shifting my posture, I felt lighter and more open.

From this new posture, I suddenly said, "I'm grateful that the company wasn't battling me to replace the floor in the first place. I'm grateful they took responsibility for the problem and were willing to replace the material and reinstall it at their own cost. That is a big relief for a floor that cost $10,000!"

The next practice is designed to support your heart rate in leveling out, which in turn will help you think more clearly and respond more effectively.

Practice #10.5: Heart-Centered Gratitude

You can do this practice seated or lying down.

You can also find a recording of this practice on my website at www.brittanyhopkins.com/heart.
First, read through the practice and have a timer set for two minutes.

1. Place one hand flat against your chest and close your eyes.
2. Imagine that you could breathe into your heart. Take a few breaths, imagining you are sending the air to the heart space.
3. When you are settled into breathing, bring to mind an experience that you've had that filled you with happiness or joy.
4. In your mind, time travel back to that experience and allow yourself to be fully immersed in it again. What do you see and hear? Is there anyone with you? Etc.

5. Stay in the feelings of that experience until the timer goes off. If you have the time and want to stay longer, feel free to do so.

Afterward, check in to see how you feel physically, mentally, and emotionally. How has this practice shifted your state of being?

Is there anything else you can authentically feel grateful for at this moment? It doesn't have to be about the drama situation you're working on. You can start small, like being grateful for the basic comforts around you (a roof over your head, nature, electricity), and work your way up to more meaningful things like friends, family, or your health. And if there's something about the drama situation you can be grateful for, go for it!

Now that you're tapped into the energy of gratitude and can breathe a little freer, it's time to get curious and see what's possible.

Just two more practices for getting out of The Drama Triangle.

The Drama of a Bubbling Yoga Floor, Getting Curious

After experiencing more lightness and openness after being grateful, I had an aha moment. I thought, *I wonder if there is a way to not close the business for a week and still have the floor replaced?*

The situation was happening in July, and our fifth business anniversary was coming up in a month. I started the yoga studio in August 2014 with free yoga in the park. It's hot in Colorado in August—perfect for outdoor classes.

What if instead of closing, we did a week-long celebration with free yoga at the park down the street? Everyone could invite friends and family, and after the celebration, we'll return to the studio with a fresh, bubble-free floor and an energized community.

149

That lightbulb idea was only possible because I went through these practices, stepped out of the drama, and opened myself to curiosity.

I still smile when I remember that aha moment and am excited for your discoveries as you practice curiosity with your situation.

Practice #10.6: Get Curious

Starting a sentence with "I wonder" can open up possibilities in a way that rigid statements like "What were they thinking?" cannot. When we say, "What were they thinking?" we focus on frustration and judgment. But if we shift to "I wonder what they were thinking," it opens us to curiosity and, often, compassion.

Set a timer for two minutes and fill in the blank after "I wonder..." continuously until the timer goes off.

The Drama of a Bubbling Yoga Floor, Claiming Responsibility

Since I created space for new possibilities in the flooring situation, it was easier for me to take responsibility for my role in the drama. I accepted that Brandi played the victim and persecutor in the drama and invited others to rescue me. I saw that not finding gratitude from the start for the flooring company's willingness to take responsibility and replace the floor for free was holding up the process and causing stress for me and those around me.

Claiming responsibility is key to stepping fully out of The Drama Triangle and reclaiming your power as a creator. Now that you've worked through your situation, it's time to get real.

This next practice may be a little uncomfortable, but it's worth it.

Practice #10.7: Claim Responsibility

Is there anything for you to take responsibility for in your situation? Can you call out your ego for its role in defending one of The Drama Triangle positions?

Examples: Maybe it started with a small mistake that snowballed into something bigger. Perhaps you're not admitting something to yourself or others, and it's holding you back. Maybe you saw the problem coming but didn't feel brave enough to make the necessary changes or voice your needs. Or maybe there's an uncomfortable feeling you're not ready to accept—whether it's sadness, anger, or fear.

Pro tip: A pillow can be an excellent tool to help process and release emotions. Talk to the pillow, cry into it, scream or yell into it, or even hit/throw it—no harm done to you or your surroundings.

Now that you've either claimed responsibility for something (or not!), let's move on to the powerful practice of letting go, so you can make space for creation in your life.

The Drama of a Bubbling Yoga Floor, Letting Go

A few days after deciding to do the yoga studio anniversary celebration in the park, I was still feeling a twinge of resentment. To let the resentment go, I journaled to see what I was holding on to.

I wrote: *I'm holding on to resentment for the floor bubbling in the first place. I'm holding on to the persecutor mindset—that it should all go my way—and only my way. I'm holding on to the feeling that I will lose business in this process. If I let all of that go, life could look and feel lighter. It could look and feel softer. It could look and feel more playful. It could look and feel like there are options.*

And then I asked myself three times, *Am I willing to give up the things I'm holding on to?* And my answer was "Maybe" all three times.

To honor the process of letting go, I wrote out the following and then sat up tall to say it out loud.

Right now, I let go of resentment.
Right now, I let go of needing things to go my way.
Right now, I let go of the fear of losing business.

And then, to set myself up for success, I wrote in my journal:

I'm present to the possibility of feeling calm.
I'm present to the possibility of options.
I'm present to the possibility of growth.

Now you try!

Practice #10.8: Let Go

1. Set a timer for two minutes and repeatedly answer the following question until the timer goes off: **What are you holding on to about this situation?**

   (It's important to use the entire two minutes, even if it's uncomfortable and you find yourself saying the same thing over and over again.)

2. Reset the timer for another two minutes and repeatedly answer: **What could life look and feel like if you let go of what you are holding on to?**

3. **Answer the following question three times to see if you are clear.**

   Are you willing to let go of the things you're holding on to?

   Yes, No, Maybe

   Are you willing to let go of the things you're holding on to?

   Yes, No, Maybe

Are you willing to let go of the things you're holding on to?

Yes, No, Maybe

4. **If your answer was yes, say it out loud or write it out three times, filling in the blank with the same thing, or something new, each time:**

Right now, I let go of...
Right now, I let go of...
Right now, I let go of...

5. **If you answered no or maybe, pretend it was a yes and say it out loud or write it out three times:**

Right now, I let go of...
Right now, I let go of...
Right now, I let go of...

6. **Set the timer for another two minutes and fill in the blank repeatedly:**

I'm present to the possibility of...
I'm present to the possibility of...
I'm present to the possibility of...

Hopefully, you were able to let go of some things.

Writing them down allows you to celebrate progress as you move forward.

Now that you've gained insight from the practices in this chapter, it's time to take action. One last practice to solidify your discoveries and hold yourself accountable.

The Drama of a Bubbling Yoga Floor, Accountability

To turn my discoveries into momentum, I set some actionable baby steps in my journal:

I will call and schedule the floor repair right now.

I will tell the team about the anniversary week of free yoga in the park via group chat today.

I will create the marketing for the free week by Friday.

Take a moment to ground yourself in your commitment. This is where your growth becomes real. Write it down, say it out loud, and take the first step toward action.

Practice #10.9: Accountability

Can you do something with the awareness you've gained? If so, commit to the next step you can take and give yourself a firm deadline. Don't let this newfound clarity slip away—hold yourself to it.

I will... (state your action step)

by... (set a specific calendar date)

Where do You Camp?

After learning about The Drama Triangle and Empowerment Dynamic, people tend to find themselves in one of a few camps, each representing a different stage of self-awareness and growth.

Camp #1 consists of those who deny any role in life's drama. In their minds, everything is fine, life is smooth, and there's nothing to address. These people might have fires burning all around them but are either unaware—or in complete denial. They're not the type who would typically pick up a book like this because, from their perspective, there's simply nothing wrong.

Camp #2 is where many of us reside. People in this camp see themselves in the drama and can make shifts relatively quickly. They acknowledge when they've slipped into The Drama Triangle, recognize that it's uncomfortable or awkward, and then consciously work to step out of it. Their lives aren't without challenges or upsets, but they have developed the tools to shift into The Empowerment Dynamic, albeit with some effort.

Camp #3 is made up of individuals who fully realize they're entrenched in the drama. They see the patterns, and understand they're causing or running from the drama, but feel trapped—unable to break free. They have spent life so deeply entangled in The Drama Triangle that it feels almost impossible to escape. These people are acutely aware of the drama but find themselves cycling through it repeatedly.

I often find myself fluctuating between Camp #2 and Camp #3. Most days, I live in Camp #2—I can recognize when I've slipped into drama roles, and with some reflection and effort, I shift back into The Empowerment Dynamic. It's not always graceful, and it can be awkward, but I'm able to catch myself and make the necessary adjustments to move forward.

But there are days when I land squarely in Camp #3. When I'm tired, stressed, or overwhelmed, I can get stuck in the drama, feeling like I'm caught in a loop, unable to find a way out. When I'm in this space, it's a clear signal that I need to reach out for support. Depending on the situation, I'll call a friend who understands these tools, seek guidance from my mindset coach, or schedule time with my therapist. Knowing when and how to ask for help is crucial. Leaning on my support system is often what helps me step out of the drama and back into empowerment.

This journey is much like the dance between our ego and higher selves. Sometimes, our ego, with all its fears and limiting beliefs, takes the lead, pulling us deeper into the drama. Other times, our higher self steps in, offering clarity, strength, and a way out. The key is recognizing who's leading the dance at any given moment and consciously using the tools we've been given to allow the higher self to take over when we find ourselves stuck.

I share this because I want you to know it's okay to be wherever you are on this journey. Whether you see yourself in Camp #1, #2, or #3—or bouncing between them as I do—your willingness to stay in the process matters.

> This isn't a journey about perfection; it's about progress. Like in a dance, it's not about getting the steps *right*—but about staying in the movement, adjusting as needed, and trusting that your higher self will gracefully take the lead when you need it most.

Action Steps for Chapter 4

This chapter's action steps encourage you to try the practices introduced on The Drama Triangle and The Empowerment Dynamic. The intention is for you to actively apply these practices to a drama you're currently experiencing with yourself, someone else, or a situation.

By engaging with these practices, you'll discover that you can gently and compassionately take the lead back from your ego self, allowing your higher self to step in and guide you as the creator of your life.

Tools for shifting out of The Drama Triangle and into The Empowerment Dynamic:

- Practice #9: What Does Your Ego Tend to Say in Drama?
- Practice #10.1: Identify Your Drama
- Practice #10.2: Exaggerate Your Current Attitude
- Practice #10.3: What if...
- Practice #10.4: Drastically Change Your Posture and Breathe on Purpose

- Practice #10.5: Heart-Centered Gratitude
- Practice #10.6: Get Curious
- Practice #10.7: Claim Responsibility
- Practice #10.8: Let Go
- Practice #10.9: Accountability

In Summary

The next time you feel resentment, judgment, powerlessness, or an overall sense of being unsettled, it's likely your ego self is playing one of the three roles in The Drama Triangle. When you recognize that you've drifted into drama, notice it without adding more drama or fuss. Use one or more of the tools from this chapter to shift yourself above the line into The Empowerment Dynamic, where peace and presence await.

Introduce this chapter and its concepts to a close friend, coworker, or family member so you can practice noticing and shifting from a victim mindset to a creator mindset, from persecutor to challenger, and rescuer to coach. The more you practice moving from The Drama Triangle to The Empowerment Dynamic, the more peace and clarity you'll bring into your life and relationships.

Moving Forward

Just one more chapter to go! In the next chapter, I'll invite you to reflect on the gifts of your ego self. You'll get clear on the areas you naturally lead in your life as your higher self because you feel and are more competent. I'll also invite you to try on a seven-day self-care challenge as a way to increase the odds of harnessing your ego for good in the dance of your life. From there, I'll send you off with all the time and space you need to practice showing up in life more intentionally, creating a beautiful dance where your higher self takes the lead, and your ego self adds its unique flourishes that make the dance fun and interesting.

CHAPTER 5

The Ongoing Journey

Before we dive into this last chapter, take a moment to reflect on your progress thus far. It takes courage to examine yourself this way—well done!

Becoming more present to yourself might leave you feeling a mix of emotions—good, bad, or somewhere in between. It's important to remember that the full range of emotions is not only normal, but also a sign of your humanity. It can be disorienting and challenging at first, but it's part of the process and worth it.

Your ego self is not going anywhere, and that's okay. It's a necessary part of the human experience. Remember, while your ego self can lead to reactive and sometimes negative behaviors, it also serves essential functions that contribute to your survival, identity, motivation, and overall growth.

Before you can harness your ego for good,
you must become fully present and find
compassion and gratitude for what that part
of yourself is trying to accomplish in life.

What you've discovered thus far:

Who you are: You now see that you have an ego self along for the ride no matter what. It helps you by giving clues about how and why you show up in the world the way you do. This awareness allows you to take action on purpose instead of reacting unconsciously. [Chapters 1 and 2]

How you interact with your ego self: Your ego gets stuck with limiting beliefs and uses ego statements to try to feel better and more in control of a situation. You can flip the narrative with empowered statements, and by becoming aware of your patterns and defaults. [Chapter 3]

How your ego and higher self interact in life: You've learned that your ego occasionally plays the roles of victim, persecutor, or rescuer in The Drama Triangle. Recognizing these roles allows you to consciously shift into creator, challenger, or coach in The Empowerment Dynamic. [Chapter 4]

This final chapter is about embracing and building competency. First, I will remind you why your ego is good and necessary and offer a few additional golden nuggets as daily habits. Then, I will close with a seven-day self-care routine to set yourself up for success in harnessing your ego for good while letting your higher self take the lead.

Reminder: Your Ego is Good and Necessary

With all the examples we've seen of our egos leading us to reactive or unhelpful behaviors, we must remember that the ego itself is not inherently bad. It plays several essential roles in our lives. Let's revisit some of the positive aspects of the ego from Chapters 1 and 2 to appreciate how it supports our survival, growth, and relationships.

1. **Survival Mechanism:** The ego helps us navigate the physical world, make decisions that protect us, and meet our basic

needs. It's the part of us that responds to danger and takes action to secure resources.

2. **Identity Formation:** The ego is essential in forming our identity. It helps us understand our place in the world. This self-awareness is necessary for personal growth and development.

3. **Motivation and Drive:** The ego often drives ambition, competitiveness, and the desire for achievement. These traits can motivate us to set goals, strive for success, and overcome obstacles.

4. **Learning and Growth:** Experiencing ego-driven behaviors, such as pride, jealousy, or anger, can provide valuable learning opportunities. By becoming aware of these feelings, we can understand their origin and harness them for personal growth and self-improvement.

5. **Social Functioning:** The ego helps us navigate social interactions and relationships. It allows us to understand social norms, communicate effectively, and develop empathy. Without it, we might struggle to connect with others and build meaningful relationships.

6. **Contrast to Higher Consciousness:** The ego provides a contrast to our higher self. By recognizing and understanding the ego, we can aspire to use it creatively in life. This contrast can enhance the human experience.

As you've learned, when your ego takes the lead, you may become reactive because of the crucial functions it has played in your survival, identity formation, motivation, and social functioning—which are good things!

How Brandi Helps Me

People who've met me might be surprised to hear that I'm generally a shy person. When I'm new to a group, I stay on the edges, surveying the scene while Brandi figures out how I fit in. Once I understand the dynamics, Brandi helps me make appropriate talking points, sometimes with a silly joke or by stepping up to lead when needed.

Brandi learned to be hypervigilant as a kid, which, as an adult, often feels like intuition when I interact with other people. Brandi is great at reading body language and voice tone shifts, helping me know what to say or ask so others feel comfortable.

Looking back on my early days as a yoga teacher, I can see how Brandi added an abundance of fun flair to my classes. The clever jokes, creative sequences, and spot-on playlists were all part of what made the Container Collective Yoga community thrive so quickly.

Those early classes brought attention to Brandi's humor, sarcasm, and opinions about what poses I liked or didn't like. There was lots of talking about how the poses felt in my body, and the focus of the classes was pushing the students to do *more*.

As I've gained competence and confidence in teaching yoga, my classes have become less of a "Brandi show." Now, when I teach, it's a partnership with my students.

Before each class, Brandi eagerly thinks, *What yoga wisdom are you going to bestow upon the students today?* I giggle and smile because it makes sense to feel proud—I've put a lot of time and effort into studying yoga. But rather than shame that part of myself for being arrogant, I gently thank her for her confidence in my teaching. I remind Brandi that I will not be bestowing anything during the class. I will simply be sharing a spiritual intention I've been exploring in my life and a physical focus I've been practicing on my mat. I trust that students will take what resonates and leave the rest.

Thanks to Brandi's drive to continuously improve, I've steadily been working on the craft of teaching yoga for twenty years. Ninety-nine percent of the time, I stand steady in front of a class as my higher self, focusing on the students' needs and experiences. I listen to Brandi's suggestions, filter them through my conscious awareness, and deliver a class in a way that is uniquely me. This balance between Brandi and my higher self makes my classes effective and authentic.

Balancing the ego with the higher self as you dance through life allows you to navigate the world effectively with levity.

Try this next practice to see what gifts your ego brings to your life.

Practice #11: Reflecting on the Gifts of Your Ego

List examples of how your ego contributes to your life. You could look back to the letter you wrote to your ego in Chapter 2, since one of the prompts in Practice #4 invited you to acknowledge what your ego has given you. I circle back on this now because, having been through the processes in the book, you may have new awareness.

Examples:

- **Ambition and Drive:** Your ego may have motivated you to achieve goals or overcome obstacles in your life.
- **Humor:** Your ego may use humor to help you connect with others, lighten situations, and even cope with challenging moments.
- **Creativity and Expression:** Your ego may have helped you express through art, music, writing, or other creative outlets.
- **Social Confidence:** Your ego may have given you the ability to navigate social situations, make connections, or lead others.

As you reflect, acknowledge the positive contributions your ego has made while staying open to ways you can continue to integrate and balance these gifts with your higher self leading the dance.

. . . .

"When you know better, do better."
—MAYA ANGELOU

. . . .

Now that I know better, everyone who works with me gets to meet both Brittany and Brandi. Rather than hide her and pretend I'm the perfect yogi—I introduce that part of myself as soon as it's appropriate. Then, I can spend more time leading classes, trainings, workshops, and retreats as my higher self and let Brandi sprinkle in her flourishes in healthy ways. After all, she has helped me get to where I am, and she knows how to make someone giggle if needed.

The Ego and Competency

Keeping in mind that Brandi would like to be the star of the show, it's an interesting exercise to reflect on when, where, and why Brandi tries to take the lead in certain parts of my day-to-day life. It seems obvious to me now, but it has taken me a minute to realize:

- My higher self tends to take the lead, allowing my ego to add flair, in the areas where I have more practice and focused training—where I feel more capable and competent.
- My ego tends to take the lead, tuning out my higher self, in areas where I have less experience or things change rapidly, where I feel less capable and incompetent.

Example of feeling competent: Because I have two decades of practice and experience in teaching yoga and ten years of practice and experience leading yoga teacher trainings, my higher self takes the lead and lets Brandi offer some lighthearted jokes here and there. Even if I've been up all night with a teething baby, I can show up to teach a class or lead a training as my higher self. I feel competent—not out of arrogance, but from the fact I've been honing my craft since 2004. Brandi doesn't take the lead as often in that area of my life.

Example of feeling incompetent: I have ADHD that went undiagnosed until I was forty-three. Before I had kids, I seemed to manage, creating workarounds for my brain fairly well.

Now that I have two kids under age seven, I feel significantly less competent at managing my brain as they grow and change at the speed of light. So, if I'm tired from being up all night with a teething baby, and am responsible for the kids all weekend, I'm more likely to feel incompetent since I have less years of practice in parenting humans who have big feelings and strong opinions. So Brandi says things like, *You should be better at this. Why can't you get your act together?* I can clearly see (and hear) Brandi as she feeds the limiting beliefs that I'm not good enough and that I'm a failure.

However, when I'm feeling mentally healthy, I can stop myself before I react by unconsciously overworking, trying to manipulate to gain control, or feeling overwhelmed and looking for cookies or a chocolate bar.

So, what do we do with the ego in moments of struggle? There are so many options and possibilities. I'll highlight three of them here:

1. Keep doing life how you've always done it, unconsciously letting the ego take the lead.

2. Use any or all of the tools in this book to see the ego and step out of default, letting the higher self take the lead.

3. Build competency through practice in the areas where you want the higher self to lead more often.

Use this next practice to understand where, when, and how your ego deals with feelings of incompetence.

Practice #12: The Dance of Competency

Part 1: Competency Awareness

In your journal/workbook:

1. **Take a deep breath, and check in with yourself physically, mentally, and emotionally.**

   "Right now, I feel _____" (relaxed, tired, energized, tense, calm, happy, etc.).

   Then, notice if you feel any resistance to your feelings. If there's resistance, fill in the blank. "It makes sense that you feel _____ because _____."

2. **What area(s) of your life do you find your *higher self* taking the lead more often because of feelings of more competence?** Your ego may also be present, but it's the higher self that has you spending more time in *action* rather than *reaction*.

3. **What area(s) of your life do you find your *ego self* taking the lead more often because of your feelings of incompetence in those areas?** Your higher self may be present, but the ego self has you spending more time in *reaction* rather than *action*.

Breathing Break: *Pause to let your thoughts settle before you continue.*

Part 2: Competency and Limiting Beliefs

1. **Are there limiting beliefs that you aren't good enough, stupid, not worthy, or something else present in the area(s) of your life where you feel less competent?** They may be actual words out loud, or they may be internal feelings.

2. **In the area(s) you feel less competent, does your ego self use statements like: "You/I should know or be better," "This is stupid," "Screw you," or "Screw this!" "It doesn't even matter," or something else?** They may be actual words out loud, or they may be internal feelings. **If so, what are they?**

3. **What would be possible if you noticed the limiting beliefs and ego statements as they show up?**

DANCING WITH OUR SELVES

4. **If limiting beliefs are present, say the following aloud or in your head.**

   - "I see and acknowledge that you feel [Insert the limiting belief]."

   - "That is a story or lie you made up when I was _____ years old."

   - "Right now, I choose to create myself as _____." [Insert how you want to feel/be. Could be the literal opposite of the limiting belief, or something else.].

Breathing Break: *Pause and take a moment to let these reframing thoughts sink in.*

Part 3: Navigating Competence using The Drama Triangle and The Empowerment Dynamic

1. **Does your ego feel like a victim, rescuer, or persecutor in the area(s) where you feel less competent?**

2. **What would be possible if you exaggerated your current reality, played the "What if" game, dramatically changed your posture, or practiced gratitude?**

3. **Where can you claim responsibility for the incompetence?** Have you not studied enough, allowed time to practice a skill, or given yourself enough time to rest? Maybe you spend time doom-scrolling social media instead of going to bed.

4. **Is there a way to set yourself up for success with goal setting or hiring support for accountability?**

Breathing Break: *Take a deep breath, close your eyes, and allow everything you've worked through to integra*te.

The higher self recognizes that we're having a human experience that includes the full range of emotions and feelings—especially as we build our competency in various areas of life.

There can be just as much beauty in the "hard"
things as in the easy and joyful moments.
By embracing the full spectrum of our
experiences, we open ourselves to deeper
understanding, growth, and, ultimately,
a richer, more fulfilling dance of life.

Any time you feel your ego self start to take the lead, you can revisit the previous practice of reflecting on your ego's gifts to support you in moving through your ego's reaction. You can also integrate conscious daily actions to set yourself up for successful higher self leadership.

Daily Practices and Choices

Being human can be hard work! There's work to be done, people to care for, possibly kids to feed and shuttle around, friends to support, a home with laundry, groceries, and dirt, maybe a car or two, and a yard to maintain. The lists go on and on. Where is there time to shower, let alone meditate, and exercise?

I recently had one of those mornings where everything felt like a marathon. Vinni had been up multiple times the night before, and I was exhausted. As soon as the sun came up, Brandi convinced me to check my emails from my phone. To her surprise and delight, one of the first messages I read stressed me out, and instead of pausing for my morning gratitude practice, I headed straight for coffee and told myself, *I'll meditate after the baby goes down for a nap.*

After chasing Vinni around all morning, I put her in the crib, but instead of meditating or taking a few minutes to breathe, Brandi pushed me right into work mode. I spent the whole napping window struggling through my to-do list, because *obviously* I didn't have time for self-care.

By midday, I felt overwhelmed, frustrated, and disconnected. I hadn't given myself any space to check in with my feelings or take care of myself, and it showed. I was sarcastic with my husband when he called to check in—fully entrenched in Brandi's victim role. I didn't seem likely I'd last the day without a Brandi meltdown.

Then, something shifted at the start of Vinni's second nap, midafternoon. My higher self gently reminded me I had a choice. I didn't need hours of meditation or a sixty-minute yoga practice to feel better—I just needed a few minutes to breathe.

Thankfully, I listened to my higher self, lit a candle, sat down for five minutes, and simply followed my breath in and out. That small choice to check in, to say to myself:

Right now, physically, I'm feeling tired.
Mentally, I feel cluttered. Emotionally, I feel anxious.
It makes sense that I feel that way.

Followed by five minutes of: *I'm breathing in...I'm breathing out...* on repeat.

This choice to shift made a world of difference. Afterward, I felt calmer, more grounded, and ready to approach the rest of my day with more compassion for myself.

> Even on hard days, we have choices. Choosing to pause and breathe intentionally can shift the entire day. It's not about doing life perfectly—it's about doing what you can with what you have.

Sometimes, all it takes is a small reminder from my higher self to refocus on what truly matters: putting my oxygen mask on first so I can truly be of service to others.

> When we take our attention off *what we don't want* and put it on *what we do want*, we can see more possibilities and choices.

Some Possibilities and Choices I get to Make Every Day:

Before I even get out of bed, I know I can choose to reach for my phone and immediately start checking texts, emails, or social media posts that I "missed" while sleeping.

I also know I can take a few moments to breathe intentionally, check how I'm feeling physically and mentally, and notice what I'm grateful for. I can even fill in the blank with, "Today I'm open to the possibility of..."

After getting out of bed, I have another choice: I could let caffeine be the first thing I put in my body, or I could drink a glass of water first. Then once the caffeine kicks in and the baby goes down for a nap, I face the temptation of immediately diving into work mode. And, I could also choose to put my favorite cushion in the middle of the kitchen floor, light a candle, burn some incense, and meditate.

The weather offers yet another crossroads. I could let it determine whether I move my body, or I could simply dress intelligently for the weather, put the baby into the stroller, and take a ten- to twenty-minute walk around the neighborhood. On days when a walk isn't possible, I can ask for support from my husband or mom with the baby while I move my body on the stationary bike or yoga mat.

Some days, Brandi chooses all her favorite options. On other days, Brandi and my higher self take turns, each making different choices to keep the day flowing. Every choice feels easier if I feel supported in the process.

What Does Support Look Like for You?

One thing that helps us make choices to feel our best is having support. Support might look like a grown-up sticker chart on the fridge, having a friend check in with you on your goals, or being part of a larger community that wants to feel good in similar ways, like joining a small yoga studio or gym, adult kickball league, etc.

When my ego is leading and resisting, it can feel like life is happening to me. It helps me to be in a community with people who support me as a creator and remind me that life is happening for me.

One way I do that is by inviting others to join me in a wellness routine to kick-start healthy habits. The following practice is a thirty-minute seven-day self-care routine that you can do alone or with a friend. Anyone can join, even if they haven't read the book or don't own a yoga mat!

Practice #13: Seven-Day Self-Care Routine

Here's an outline of a simple seven-day self-care routine that I use in my own life to cultivate daily habits for well-being. If you're anything like me, it can bring you closer to leading your life as your higher self.

Be sure to visit www.brittanyhopkins.com/self-care for free videos that accompany this program.

What You'll Need:
- **Essentials:** An open mind and a willing attitude.

- **Optional:** A yoga mat, straight-back chair, yoga blocks, and a journal or journaling app.

How to Begin:

1. **Commit:** Dedicate seven days to this practice.

2. **Morning Routine:**
   - Start each morning with a glass of water.
   - Journaling session (three to five minutes) using the following three prompts:
     - "Right now, I'm feeling..."
     - "I'm grateful for..."
     - "Today, I'm open to the possibility of feeling..."

3. **Daily Meditation:** Set aside five minutes (preferably in the morning) for meditation using a timer, a meditation app, resources from my website, or YouTube.

4. **Physical Practice:** Schedule a twenty-minute mindful movement practice each day—whether it's yoga, a walk, or any other activity that keeps you present.

How to End the Week:

1. **Morning Reflection:** Reflect on your week by writing three to five discoveries from your week of self-care practices.

2. **Extended Meditation:** Complete a ten-minute meditation session.

3. **Gentle Movement:** Allow your body to rest with gentle movement or a Yin Yoga session. Consider taking an intentional nap or enjoying restorative practices available on my website.

Invitation: This is not a seven-day commitment to add to your to-do list. It's an intentional way of living your life. Some days, you may have more time to move your body or meditate. On the flip side, vacations, holidays, and illnesses will happen and can pull you out of your routine. Don't worry! You now understand how to dance with your ego, and can stop any shame spirals and simply begin again as soon as possible.

Remember, it's not about achieving perfection; it's about making continuous, conscious efforts to take the lead in your life as your higher self and dance with your ego.

. . . .

"Our greatest glory is not in never falling, but in rising each time we fall." —CONFUCIUS

. . . .

Give Yourself Grace

It's about Progress, not Perfection: The practices and insights shared in this book are not one-time fixes but ongoing processes that evolve with you.

Embrace the journey of continuous self-discovery.

The Highs Get Higher, and the Lows Get Higher: Imagine a roller coaster climbing the side of a mountain. There are peaks and drops, but as the ride progresses, the highs reach greater heights, and even the lows rise above where they began. This is the natural ebb and flow of life.

As you learn to harness your ego and let your higher self lead, those lows could feel less overwhelming, and the highs could become even more enriching.

What if we treated life like a roller coaster— filled with thrilling ups and downs? Buckle up for safety, but remember: The choice is yours. You can hold on tight, clinging to fear,

or throw your hands in the air, surrender to
the journey, and just maybe...enjoy the ride.

Practice Nonattachment: As your higher self, you can feel the full range of emotions. It's either your resistance to emotions or your attachment to them that sends you into ego reactions.

As your higher self, you can feel happy. It's the *attachment* to keeping that happiness as a feeling forever that makes it ego-driven. You can feel sad and still be your higher self. It's resistance to feeling sadness that comes from your ego self.

How to practice nonattachment:

- Do a day in the life of you.
- Notice the ego trying to take the lead or drive the car.
- Become aware of how you're feeling and see if it makes sense that you feel that way.
- Let go of resistance or attachment to the feelings.

I'm Open to the Possibility of: Some days, my ego is very attached and tries to control the flow of life. I use the fill-in-the-blank practice, "I'm open to the possibility of..." to loosen my mental and emotional grip on how I think something should go or how I want it to go. Try it whenever you find yourself stuck in attachment.

Simply Notice and Begin Again (without a "should-show"): When you've noticed that you've slid off course into ego reaction, remember: Competency is built one moment at a time. Acknowledge if you've fallen into old habits and patterns, take a deep breath, say your empowered statement, and begin again.

It's not magic; it's just practice.

Support and Accountability: Create a support system to help you stay accountable to your journey. This could be a friend, a community group, or an online forum.

Surround yourself with people who
share your commitment to letting their
higher selves take the lead in life.

Share Your Journey: Talk about your experiences with others who are also on a journey of self-discovery. Sharing your insights and challenges can provide additional insights.

Celebrate Progress: Acknowledge and celebrate your progress, no matter how small—recognizing that personal growth is an ongoing journey.

Guess what—there's a community built around these ideas and practices! Join my community and participate in live online and in-person classes, trainings, workshops, and retreats. You can explore all of the additional resources on my website.

Action Steps for Chapter 5

You have a unique way of showing up in the world, thanks to your ego. When you're healthy and balanced, that's a good thing. In the areas where you feel less competent and your ego is leading, you can use the tools in this book to support you as you build competency.

With the seven-day self-care routine, you can make daily choices to support yourself in living life like a dance rather than a battle. By incorporating a self-care routine, you build a strong foundation for embracing your ego and allowing your higher self to lead. This journey requires ongoing practice, awareness, and compassion, and it's a path toward greater authenticity, purpose, and joy.

- Practice #11: Reflecting on the Gifts of Your Ego Self
- Practice #12: The Dance of Competency
- Practice #13: Seven-Day Self-Care Challenge

May you live your life with curiosity and compassion! Embrace the dance between your ego and higher self, knowing that each step, graceful or faltering, is a part of your unique journey.

Continue to practice, reflect, and grow—while allowing your higher self to guide you toward a life of authenticity, purpose, and joy.

THANK YOU

First, to *you*! You could have spent your time in countless ways, yet you chose to read through these pages with me. The gratitude I feel for you, the reader, is beyond words.

To my husband, Adam, without you, this book wouldn't have happened, at least not yet. Thank you for lovingly redirecting me whenever my ego tried to chicken out of the process. You've spent countless hours talking through concepts and stories with me, and (even better) you live the practices with me in real time every day. Thank you for loving me—Brandi and all. Perhaps the adventures of Brandi and Alex will inspire a comic book one day!

To Pop, Jennifer, and Mom—who have been my cheerleaders throughout life. Thank you for loving and supporting me through my wild ideas. Thank you for modeling what hard work, commitment, and follow-through look like. I've taken so many leaps in life because of the comforting thought: *If this doesn't work out, I can always move back home.*

To Mom/Gramma Deb—the world's best stage mom. Never overbearing, always encouraging, and ready with a safety pin or flower arrangement. With your love and willingness to watch the kids, I've been able to run a yoga business, lead trainings, and pour my heart into sharing the practices of yoga. Without you, who knows when this book would have been finished—if ever.

To Dr. Deb, thank you for being the very first person to read the draft of this book. Your generosity in giving feedback and willingness to sit with my early ideas meant the world to me, and I'm so grateful.

To my friends—who have joined me in these conversations and tirelessly listened to my processes over the years.

To Mollie—thank you for saying yes to this yoga journey, which is what brought us together in the first place. Your friendship has been one of the most beautiful and unexpected gifts. We prove that living in the same time zone is not a prerequisite for deep friendship. When I was deep in the trenches of this book-writing adventure, you stepped in and offered to share your skills as an editor, offering line-by-line feedback. This book is so much stronger because of your sharp eye, thoughtful suggestions, and generous spirit. I'm so grateful you believe in me, and this project. Thank you for being such a steady and supportive presence through it all.

To Jamie—how would I even be standing without you? You've laughed and cried with me through motherhood. Your friendship has been a lifeline in the hardest and most joyful moments of these last ten years. You remind me that I don't have to do it alone, and I'm beyond thankful for that...and you!

To all of my teachers, formal and informal, thank you for challenging me to live into my potential, even when I couldn't see it myself. Every lesson you've imparted has helped me grow—not just as a teacher and leader but as a person. You've given me the tools to walk this path with authenticity and grace.

To Heather—my woo-woo guide. I'll never forget the deep breath you took on our very first call. You knew the work ahead for me and stayed through it all. You challenged me in ways I had no idea I needed and showed me that I could believe in myself.

To Alyse and Ellen—my professional trampolines. You each played such integral roles in catching me when I fell and bounced me back up when I needed extra support. Your guidance has been priceless. Thank you for being there when I needed you through the writing process and beyond.

To my son, Isaac—thank you for surprising me with your existence. I see how I was hiding from myself before you showed up, and thanks to you, I've remembered what was needed to heal and grow. This book would not exist if you hadn't decided to join the party.

To my daughter, Vinni—the baby girl the Universe told me about when I was packing up my life to move to Beijing in 2013. Who would've guessed you'd arrive ten years later to rock my world in the best way possible?

Last but not least, thank you to every single student who has allowed me to guide you through a class, training, workshop, or retreat over the last twenty years. Your courage, commitment, questioning, and curiosity have inspired me every day of my teaching journey. Thank you for being my gurus!

REFERENCES

Sir Isaac Newton once said, "If I have seen further, it's by standing on the shoulders of giants." It's essential to recognize that the concepts and ideas explored throughout this book are not unique to a single perspective or time. Much of what is now considered general knowledge in personal growth, psychology, and spirituality has evolved from centuries of exploration and inquiry into the nature of the human mind and soul.

These insights are not static but have evolved over time, shaped by the contributions of numerous thinkers and the changing cultural and intellectual landscape. The insights presented in this book are deeply rooted in the ancient wisdom of yogic philosophy from India, and the foundational work of modern psychology, particularly the contributions of Sigmund Freud, Carl Jung, and other thought leaders.

The tools and frameworks discussed here are products of the past and seeds for the future. Whether related to the interplay between the ego and higher selves, mindfulness practices, The Drama Triangle and Empowerment Dynamic, these ideas are built upon the wisdom of those who have explored them. Their research, teachings, and philosophies have helped create a foundation for modern understanding. It's our turn to continue this evolution to delve deeper into self-awareness and growth.

These ideas have become part of a shared cultural and intellectual landscape. This reference section is organized by chapter and acknowledges many sources that have inspired and informed the content. Whether from ancient spiritual traditions or modern therapeutic models, the teachings cited here have been invaluable in shaping, either directly or indirectly, this book and my personal and professional journey.

Introduction

Development of the Ego

Freud, Sigmund. *The Ego and the Id.* W.W. Norton & Company, 1923.
Erikson, Erik H. *Childhood and Society.* W.W. Norton & Company, 1950.

Higher Self and Ego Dynamics

Jung, Carl. *The Archetypes and the Collective Unconscious.* Princeton University Press, 1969.
Tolle, Eckhart. *A New Earth: Awakening to Your Life's Purpose.* Penguin Group, 2005.

Mindful Action and Presence

Singer, Michael A. *The Untethered Soul: The Journey Beyond Yourself.* New Harbinger Publications, 2007.

Ego and Internal Conflict

Freud, Sigmund. *The Ego and the Id.* W.W. Norton & Company, 1923.
Tolle, Eckhart. *The Power of Now: A Guide to Spiritual Enlightenment.* New World Library, 1997.

Chapter 1

Yamas and Niyamas (Yogic Philosophy)

Iyengar, B.K.S. *Light on Yoga.* HarperCollins, 1966.

Adele, Deborah. *The Yamas & Niyamas: Exploring Yoga's Ethical Practice.* On-Word Bound Books, 2009.

Mehrotra, Anand. *This Is That: Patanjali's Yoga Sutra for the Modern World.* Sattva Yoga Academy, 2017.

Internal Family Systems (IFS)

Schwartz, Richard C. *Internal Family Systems Therapy.* Guilford Press, 1995.

Cognitive Defusion (Acceptance and Commitment Therapy)

Hayes, Steven C., and Spencer Smith. *Get Out of Your Mind and Into Your Life: The New Acceptance and Commitment Therapy.* New Harbinger Publications, 2005.

Hayes, Steven C., Kirk D. Strosahl, and Kelly G. Wilson. *Acceptance and Commitment Therapy: The Process and Practice of Mindful Change.* Guilford Press, 2011.

Illeism (Third-Person Self-Talk)

Kross, Ethan, et al. "Self-Talk as a Regulatory Mechanism: How You Do It Matters." *Journal of Personality and Social Psychology,* vol. 106, no. 2, 2014, pp. 304–324. DOI: 10.1037/a0035173.

Ego Development and Historical Context

Freud, Sigmund. *The Ego and the Id.* W.W. Norton & Company, 1923.

Plato. *Phaedrus.* Hackett Publishing Company, 1995 (originally written in 370 B.C.E.).

Mehrotra, Anand. *This Is That - Patanjali's Yoga Sutras Padas 1 and 2.* Sattva Yoga Academy, 2020.

Name it to Tame it

Siegel, Daniel J. *The Whole-Brain Child: 12 Revolutionary Strategies to Nurture Your Child's Developing Mind.* Bantam, 2011.

Chapter 2

Kriya Yoga Meditation Technique

Mollie Busby, Meditation and Yoga Teacher Trainer E-RYT 500, RPYT, RCYT. www.MollieBusby.com

Quote: "What You Resist Persists"

Jung, Carl. *The Archetypes and the Collective Unconscious.* Princeton University Press, 1969.

Terry Real's Relational Life Therapy (Letter to Ego Self)

Real, Terry. Audible Workshop: Fierce Intimacy.

Chapter 3

Limiting Beliefs and Defying the Lie

Baptiste Institute, Level 1: Journey into Power with Baron Baptiste (Live Training), Sedona, AZ, 2013.

Baptiste, Baron. *Being of Power: The 9 Practices to Ignite an Empowered Life.* New York: Simon & Schuster, 2014.

Yogic Concepts of Ahamkara (ego) and Asmita (false identification) can be found in the Yoga Sutras.

Mehrotra, Anand. *This Is That - Patanjali's Yoga Sutras Padas 1 and 2.* Sattva Yoga Academy, 2020.

Anand Mehrotra, *That Is This: Patanjali's Yoga Sutras Padas 3 and 4.* Sattva Yoga Academy, 2021.

Adele, Deborah. *The Kleshas: Exploring the Elusiveness of Happiness.* Duluth, MN: On-Word Bound Books, 2019.

Cognitive Behavioral Therapy (CBT) and Reframing Limiting Beliefs

Beck, Aaron T., and Judith S. Beck. *Cognitive Behavior Therapy: Basics and Beyond*. 2nd ed. New York: Guilford Press, 2011.

Neuro-Linguistic Programming (NLP) and Reframing Limiting Beliefs

Andreas, Steve, and Charles Faulkner. *NLP: The New Technology of Achievement*. New York: HarperCollins, 1996.

Positive Psychology

Seligman, Martin E. P. *Flourish: A Visionary New Understanding of Happiness and Well-being*. New York: Free Press, 2011.

Spiritual Mindset Teachers

Hay, Louise L. *You Can Heal Your Life*. Carlsbad, CA: Hay House, 1984.

Robbins, Tony. *Awaken the Giant Within: How to Take Immediate Control of Your Mental, Emotional, Physical and Financial Destiny!* New York: Free Press, 2001.

Brown, Brené. *Daring Greatly: How the Courage to Be Vulnerable Transforms the Way We Live, Love, Parent, and Lead*. New York: Gotham Books, 2012.

Bernstein, Gabrielle. *The Universe Has Your Back: Transform Fear to Faith*. Carlsbad, CA: Hay House, 2016.

Baptiste, Baron. *Perfectly Imperfect: The Art and Soul of Yoga Practice*. Boulder, CO: Sounds True, 2016.

Chapter 4

The Drama Triangle and The Empowerment Dynamic®

Karpman, Stephen B. "Fairy Tales and Script Drama Analysis." Transactional Analysis Bulletin 7, no. 26 (1968): 39-43.

Center for The Empowerment Dynamic, Coaching with TED*, *The Empowerment Dynamic, with Donna Zajonc MCC (Live Training), Online, April–June 2024.

Emerald, David. *The Power of TED*:* The Empowerment Dynamic.* Bainbridge Island, WA: Polaris Publishing, 2016.

Website: The Power of TED* www.theempowermentdynamic.com

Website: Conscious Leadership Group. Accessed April 2018. https://conscious.is/resources.

Website: HeartMath Institute. Accessed June, 2024. https://www.heartmath.com.

Chapter 5

Angelou, Maya. "When You Know Better, You Do Better." *Even the Stars Look Lonesome.* Random House, 1997.

The Ego and Competency

Adele, Deborah. *The Yamas & Niyamas: Exploring Yoga's Ethical Practice.* On-Word Bound Books, 2009.

Get The Workbook For Free!

To say thank you for reading my book, I would like to give you the *Dancing with Our Selves: A Practical Guide to Harness the Ego and Live on Purpose* companion workbook 100 percent FREE!

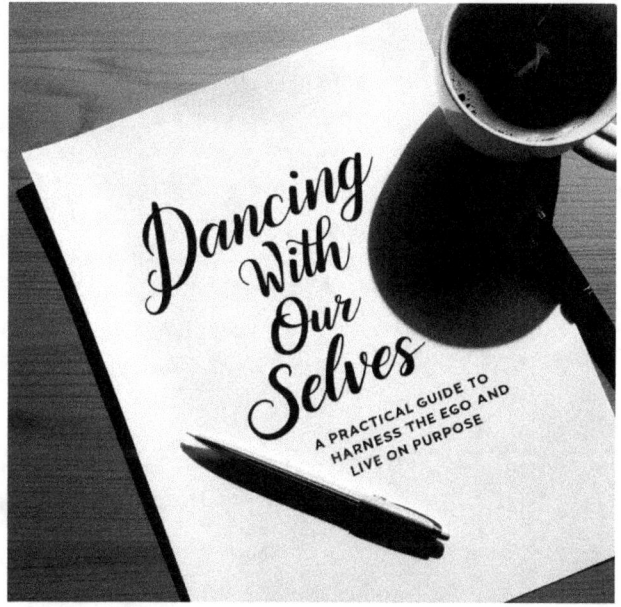

You can get a copy by visiting:
www.brittanyhopkins.com

Thank You
For Reading My Book!

Your support means the world to me. I'd love to hear
your thoughts—what resonated with you, what worked,
and how this book has impacted your journey.

My work evolves through the feedback I receive from
readers like you. Your insights not only help me grow but
also allow me to better serve others on their path.

www.brittanyhopkins.com

If you found this book valuable, please share your
thoughts in a review on Amazon. Your feedback
helps more people discover these practices and join
the dance between the ego and higher self.

With heartfelt gratitude,

www.ingramcontent.com/pod-product-compliance
Lightning Source LLC
Chambersburg PA
CBHW061750120626
46550CB00005B/1951